Developing academic library staff for future success

Developing academic library staff for future success

Edited by
Margaret Oldroyd

facet publishing

© The compilation: Margaret Oldroyd 2004
The articles: the contributors 2004

Published by
Facet Publishing
7 Ridgmount Street
London WC1E 7AE

Facet Publishing (formerly Library Association Publishing) is wholly owned by
CILIP: the Chartered Institute of Library and Information Professionals.

First published 2004

British Library Cataloguing in Publication Data
A catalogue record for this book is available from the British Library.

ISBN 1-85604-478-5

Typeset from editor's disks by Facet Publishing Production in Elegant Garamond
and Humanist 521
Printed and made in Great Britain by MPG Books Ltd, Bodmin, Cornwall.

Contents

The contributors

Moira Bent has been the Science Faculty Librarian at the University of Newcastle upon Tyne for the last six years. Her particular interests are information literacy skills and staff development. For the last eight years she has run collaborative staff development workshops (LibLearn) with other North East England university library staff. She is a member of the staff development group at Newcastle University Library. Recently, she has been instrumental in developing a staff development module for the Newcastle library staff using the Blackboard Virtual Learning Environment. The CILIP UC&R Innovation Award in 2002 allowed her to investigate the development of a collaborative staff development module, using Blackboard, with colleagues from the University of Durham. She is Chair of the UK Universities Science and Technology Librarians Group, and a member of the Royal Society of Chemistry Journals Committee, the JISC PSIgate Advisory Board and the JISC Resource Guide Advisory Board for Physical Sciences.

Sheila Corrall is Professor of Librarianship and Information Management at the University of Sheffield. Before moving to Sheffield, she spent thirteen years leading and managing university library and information services, most recently as Director of Academic Services at the University of Southampton. She worked for ten years at the British Library and five years in the public library sector. She has served on many national committees, including the British Council Library and Information Services Advisory Committee, the JISC Committee on Electronic Information, the

SCONUL Executive Board and the UK Office for Library and Information Networking Management Committee. She was the founding Chair of the Information Services National Training Organisation and first President of the Chartered Institute of Library and Information Professionals. In 2003 she received the International Information Industry Lifetime Achievement Award in recognition of her contribution to the development of the profession.

Philippa Dolphin has been Librarian of Birkbeck, University of London since 1995. She has worked at several other higher education libraries in the London area. She has been involved in collaborative staff development through the M25 Consortium of Higher Education Libraries, and was a member of the Joint M25 and University of London Staff Training and Development Group Review.

Biddy Fisher is Head of Academic Services and Development within the Learning Centre at Sheffield Hallam University. Her work involves planning and implementing the appropriate departmental response to teaching, learning and research in a large modern university. The Learning Centre has made specific challenges to staff development and training by stimulating the transition from 'traditional' information support to a contemporary learner support model in line with SHU's development of the Virtual Learning Environment.   Biddy has used her experience and her significant network of professional colleagues to inform her chapter. Maintaining her contact with new and emerging professionals is important to the integrity of her work and currently she is an External Examiner at Leeds Metropolitan University, as well as one of two new appointments of External Examiner to the CILIP Chartership Board.

Sally Neocosmos is currently Registrar and Secretary at the University of York. In a career spanning over thirty years she has held a range of senior administrative posts in five higher education institutions. She has also contributed at various times to national higher education policy development in the UK and South Africa, most recently with the Department for Education and Skills (DfES). At the time of writing this chapter she was Chief Executive of the Higher Education Staff Development Agency (HESDA).

Patrick Noon has been University Librarian at Coventry University since 1993. Before that he worked at Staffordshire and De Montfort universities. He is a former Committee member of the Personnel, Training and Education Group of CILIP and, until 2002, was Chair of SCONUL's Advisory Committee on Staffing (ACoS). While on ACoS he helped to develop and promote a strategic management course for senior staff in libraries and information services. Most recently, Pat was a member of the Steering Group for the HEFCE-funded Hybrid Information Skills for Senior Staff (HIMSS) Project.

Margaret Oldroyd is Staff and Quality Development Manager for the Department of Library Services at De Montfort University. She leads the first accredited Information and Library Services NVQ Centre in a university library and is a qualified assessor and internal verifier. The Department is recognized as an Investor in People. She is Chair of the CILIP Chartership Board, and a member of the SCONUL Advisory Committee on Staffing, for which she has led a group to produce a strategy for the development of senior library managers, especially in relation to management and leadership skills. Her Masters degree dissertation and her publications, including a previous book for Facet Publishing, exemplify her professional focus on strategic development of all staff as a key success factor for academic libraries. In her spare time, Margaret is a Federation Councillor for Soroptimist International, a world-wide organization for women in management and the professions, which views education as a key factor in addressing inequalities and poverty and thus enhancing the status of women.

Chris Powis is Learning Support Co-ordinator at University College Northampton, leading the team of Academic Librarians there. He joined UCN in 1991 as the Business Librarian, after starting his professional career at Bristol Polytechnic. Chris was one of the Development Officers for the JISC-funded Edulib Project and has subsequently delivered workshops and courses on teaching for librarians in the UK and Finland. He is a member of the ILTHE and has served on their membership committee. He supervises Chartership candidates and is a Regional Assessor for CILIP.

Margaret Weaver is Head of Library Services at St Martin's College (Lancaster). Prior to this she was the Head of User Support at the University of Central Lancashire, moving here in 2001 from the University of Huddersfield, where she was Academic Librarian for the School of Human and Health Sciences. Margaret has a keen interest in staff development and CPD activities. She was Chair of the Staff Development Group of the Accessing Lancashire Library & Information Services (ALLIS) and Chair of the West Yorkshire branch of the University College and Research Group. She has been involved with various research projects; for example she was the Project Director of the JISC-funded INHALE Project and a member of the group that won the LIRG Daphne Clark Prize in 1998 for work on centralized classification.

Jo Webb is Business, Law and Humanities Team Manager at De Montfort University in Leicester. She has been Internal Verifier for ILS NVQs since De Montfort became an Assessment Centre in 1996 and is also an Assessor. In 1990 her first published work won the Peter New prize of the Library Association's Personnel, Training and Education Group. This was a study on the qualifications and progression routes for library support staff in the UK, a topic area that continues to be of both personal and professional interest. She is Secretary of CILIP's University, College and Research Group.

Sue White is Deputy Director of Computing and Library Services (LIS) at the University of Huddersfield. She has worked in higher education and further education, and has always taken a keen interest in staff training and development. Currently she is a member of the YMLAC (Yorkshire Museums Libraries and Archives Council) Workforce Development Working Group and the Yorkshire Universities LIS Staff Development Group. She is a founder member of The Consortium: Partners in Training and Development for Libraries in Yorkshire, based at Leeds Metropolitan University, which organizes and delivers workshops for LIS staff.

Introduction

Margaret Oldroyd

Writing at the start of the new century, DeCandido stated that, while the values and purposes of academic librarianship had not changed, much else had altered as a result of technology:

> The source for the radical change in the work lives of librarians is technology: automation, telecommunications, the Internet. Not only has developing technology changed the way we do things like cataloguing and processing, it has changed the ways we think about the work we do (DeCandido, 2003, 3).

In the same year, a review of the changing roles of library professionals stressed the significance not only of technology but also of organizational development and redesign, the greater focus on team-based approaches to tasks, and the realignment of library priorities to support redefined university goals (ARL, 2000).

The urgent necessity for acquiring new skills is helpfully summarized by Garrod:

> Failure to do so, through apathy or procrastination, could amount to professional suicide … the digital era requires staff who thrive on change and who are proactive in terms of both their approach to work and their own professional development (Garrod, 1998, 244–5).

This book looks at the changing higher education library context, both what it is like now, and the contributors' views on the future. It highlights significant issues and current and future role changes, and evaluates the implications of these for skill needs and development routes. Its aim is to consider the place of staff development in the current and future strategic management of academic libraries, and so its primary intended audience is current and future library managers. All the contributors are practising managers in higher education and write within that context. However, the principles and issues that they discuss are equally relevant for library staff and managers who work in further education institutions. The contributors' comments are illustrated by drawing on their own experience and that of colleagues, and by including relevant international initiatives where appropriate.

The first four chapters of this book examine sources of change in the institutional and library environments, with particular attention being paid to the networked environment, to working in converged services and to the implications for developing the academic library managers of the future. Unlike the rest of the book, the first chapter focuses on the UK context, but raises questions that have wider relevance.

Chapters 5 and 6 analyse changing roles, development needs and routes for staff who directly promote and support learning, and for support staff. In Chapter 7 the significance of increasingly flexible patterns of working are analysed, together with the consequences for development needs and mechanisms. Chapters 8 and 9 evaluate the actual and potential uses of virtual learning environments, and regional training co-operatives for delivering training and development opportunities in the new context.

The last chapter explores the emerging role of staff development as part of a planned approach to human resource management, and its importance for achieving success in academic libraries' strategic goals.

Finally, it should be noted that the term 'academic library' covers universities and colleges of higher education, and is also understood to include the many other names used in the sector such as learning resources centre, learning centre, information centre. 'Staff' includes all staff unless an author states that they are referring to a particular group. 'Staff development' is understood to include training and continuing professional development activities.

My thanks go to all the authors who have given so generously of their time, skills and knowledge to contribute to this book. I would also like to thank my husband Robert for providing the index, and for his constant support.

References

Association of Research Libraries (2000) *Changing Roles of Library Professionals*, SPEC Kit 256, Washington, DC, ARL.

DeCandido, G. A. (2000) New Jobs for Old: librarians now, *Leading Ideas*, **14**, 1–16.

Garrod, P. (1998) Skills for New Information Professionals (SKIP): an evaluation of key findings, *Program*, **32** (3), 241–63.

Glossary

ALP	Association of Learning Providers
ANGEL	Authenticated Networked Guided Environment for Learning (project)
ANLTC	Academic and National Library Training Cooperative
ARL	Association of Research Libraries
AULIC	Avon University Libraries in Cooperation
BECTA	British Educational Communications and Technology Agency
CALIM	Consortium of Academic Libraries in Manchester
CETUS	Consortium for Educational Technology in University Systems
CILIP	Chartered Institute of Library and Information Professionals
CILS	Certificate in Information and Library Studies
CIPD	Chartered Institute of Personnel and Development
CLIP	Certificate in Information and Library Practice
CMPS	Centre for Management and Policy Studies
COLIS	Collaborative Online Learning and Information Service
COPAC	Consortium of University Research Libraries
CPD	Continuing Professional Development
CURL	Consortium of University Research Libraries

DfES	Department for Education and Skills
DLIST	Digital Library of Information Science and Technology
DTI	Department of Trade and Industry
ECDL	European Computer Driving Licence
ECU	Equality Challenge Unit
E-LIS	E-Prints in Library and Information Science
EMALINK	East Midlands Academic Libraries in Cooperation
ENTO	Employment National Training Organisation
FAIR	Focus on Access to Institutional Resources
FENTO	Further Education National Training Organisation
FERL	Further Education Resources for Learning
HEFCE	Higher Education Funding Council for England
HEI	Higher Education Institution
HERON	Higher Education Resources on the Net
HESA	Higher Education Statistics Agency
HESDA	Higher Education Staff Development Agency
HIMSS	Hybrid Information Skills for Senior Staff (project)
HND	Higher National Diploma
HRM	Human Resource Management
IATUL	International Association of Technological University Libraries
ICOLC	International Coalition of Library Consortia
ICT	Information and Communication Technology
IiP	Investors in People
ILS NVQs	Information and Library Services National Vocational Qualifications
ILTHE	Institute for Learning and Teaching in Higher Education
IMPEL	Impact on People of Electronic Libraries (project)
INHALE	Information for Nursing and Health in a Learning Environment
INSIST	Impact of NVQs in Information and Library Services on Library Staff Induction and Staff Training
ISNTO	Information Services National Training Organisation
IT	Information Technology

JISC	Joint Information Systems Committee
LIRG	Library and Information Research Group (CILIP)
LIS	Library and Information Services
LSC	Learning and Skills Council
LTSN	Learning and Teaching Support Network
MLE	Managed Learning Environment
MOSAIC	Making Sense of Information in the Connected Age
NCIHE	National Committee of Inquiry into Higher Education
NCVQ	National Council for Vocational Qualifications
NoWAL	North West Academic Libraries
NTO	National Training Organisation
NVQ	National Vocational Qualification
OPAC	Online Public Access Catalogue
OPM	Office for Public Management
PTEG	Personnel, Training and Education Group (CILIP)
QCA	Qualifications and Curriculum Authority
RAE	Research Assessment Exercise
RDN	Resource Discovery Network
RSLG	Research Support Libraries Group
SALCTG	Scottish Academic Libraries Cooperative Training Group
SCONUL	Society of College, National and University Libraries
SEDA	Staff and Educational Development Association
SINTO	Sheffield Information Organisation
SNVQ	Scottish National Vocational Qualification
SPARC	Scholarly Publishing and Academic Resources Coalition
SSC	Sector Skills Council
SSDA	Sector Skills Development Agency
SWDP	Sector Workforce Development Plan
TapIN	Training and Awareness Programme in Networks (project)
TQE	Teaching Quality Enhancement
UC&R	University, College and Research Group (CILIP)
UCEA	Universities and Colleges Employers Association

UCISA	Universities and Colleges Information Systems Association
UCoSDA	Universities and Colleges Staff Development Agency
UKeU	UK eUniversities Worldwide
UKOLN	UK Office for Library and Information Networking
UUK	Universities UK
VLE	Virtual Learning Environment
VRD	Virtual Reference Desk
WHELF	Wales Higher Education Libraries Forum
WUN	World Universities Network

1

Human resources for higher education in the 21st century: a strategic overview of development needs

Sally Neocosmos

Introduction

This strategic overview considers the changing higher education environment and workforce development issues and priorities. It highlights the role of leadership and management development and of some key institutional factors for effective continuing professional development (CPD), and ends with a brief consideration of academic library staff. While specific references are to the UK context, the issues raised are generic ones.

How often do we hear that people are our most valuable resource? This is undoubtedly true in UK higher education, a sector that, according to HESDA,[1] employs over 400,000 people (HESDA, 2001) and which routinely devotes 60% of its annual expenditure to staff-related costs (HESA, 2002). Employers who invest significant time and money in initial and continuing development and training of their staff will always claim a more highly skilled and motivated workforce than those who give it lower priority (UCoSDA, 1994, 6–9).

A serious criticism of employers, especially at times of economic difficulty, is that they are all too ready to sacrifice the training budget to make ends meet, a position that would not suggest investment decisions being made in the context of a strategic or business plan.

The Higher Education Funding Council for England (HEFCE) interim evaluation of its rewarding and developing staff initiative shows that there can be little doubt that any such false economy in higher education is a thing of the past and investment in staff development and training for all categories of staff is being afforded high priority (HEFCE, 2002). There is also growing evidence of staff development and training activities being integrated with institutions' business and strategic plans. HESDA's contacts with human resources and staff development professionals in the sector indicate that initial training and qualification is now invariably coupled with structured continuing professional development and that development needs, increasingly underpinned – for all groups of staff – by explicit statements of skills, qualifications and professional or occupational standards, are being identified in part through review and appraisal processes.

All higher education staff work in a complex environment and higher education institutions face the same business challenges as other sectors in a rapidly changing political, social, economic and technological environment. Higher education staff are many and varied and institutions can neither uphold their core academic rationale, nor provide high quality services effectively – whether to students, staff or other stakeholders – without the back-up of various teams of people, combining their respective expertise in a strategically planned environment. This is the context in which staff development and training are located in higher education today.

The higher education workforce and the changing higher education context

The higher education sector's workforce development plan (HESDA, 2001)[2] reported that 48% of the UK higher education workforce are men and 52% are women, with proportionally fewer women than men on higher salary grades. These people have contributed to significant productivity gains over the past two decades in which there has been unprecedented student growth and a declining unit of resource.

In 1999–2000 there were 1.8 million students enrolled in UK higher education and the Government has set an ambitious target of 50% of under 30 year olds participating in higher education by 2010. With this growth has come a more diverse student body: more students are over 21 when they embark on their studies, some enter higher education without traditional academic qualifications, and many study part-time or work part-time to support full-time studies. Student growth has also been accompanied by increased concentration of research funding and a more diverse sector in terms of institutional mission. This diversity looks set to increase further in the wake of the Government's White Paper on the future of higher education (DfES, 2003) with its four main strands: widening participation and fair access; enhancing excellence in learning and teaching; enhancing excellence in research; and enhancing the contribution of higher education to the economy and society. The diversity of occupations needed to support an effective higher education sector gives rise to a wide range of workforce development issues affecting the ability of the workforce as a whole to respond and adapt to change in the sector.

Workforce development issues and priorities

Successive surveys and reports (HESDA, 2002, 2001;[3] OPM 2002; Thewlis, 2001) show a sector faced with a number of workforce development issues, which are being tackled in different ways. In England, the HEFCE rewarding and developing staff initiative has raised the profile of human resource management and kick-started some fundamental changes in the sector (2002). Among various workforce development issues it is regular recruitment difficulties that gain the most public attention, but others, and particularly staff development and training, are equally vital to the continuing success of UK higher education. Stimulated by the HEFCE initiative and parallel policy aims of the other funding councils, major investments are being made in recruitment and retention of staff and in staff training and development, especially professional training, IT training, equal opportunity and diversity training and management development.[4]

Some recruitment difficulties are the direct consequence of a shortage of suitably trained and skilled workers, while others are related to structural employment factors, such as regional variations in supply and demand, or pay and conditions in the higher education sector (Thewlis, 2001). There are also a number of strategic challenges for all higher education institutions. These include diversity and equality issues, managing work–life balance, professional and/or occupational standards, and different routes to qualification or accreditation for various roles. Perhaps the issue that is set to have the most profound effect on traditional higher education structures and practices in the foreseeable future is job evaluation. This is an essential prerequisite of equal pay and has been widely welcomed in principle but its outcomes are expected to challenge some long-standing pay and grading assumptions and anomalies leading, at least in the short term, to some turbulence for institutions.

A majority of higher education institutions experience deficiency in the skills of some of their staff. Such skills gaps are indicative of particular staff development needs if skills are to remain up to date, for example in response to changing working practices and technological developments. Institutions surveyed in early 2001 reported a number of common skills gaps in relation to the different occupations in the workforce (HESDA, 2001). Most of these were for generic or transferable skills applicable in different degrees to most or all categories of staff.

The first and most widely cited skills gap found in the research for the sector workforce development plan was in management skills. This was very widely identified and, in particular, a lack of skills in project management, change management, contract management, strategic management and financial planning was highlighted. Next in importance were inadequate team working skills, including specific techniques in collaboration and co-operation for administrative staff. This was followed by a lack of information technology (IT) skills, especially basic skills for those with little experience of using IT, software and website skills for administrative and secretarial staff, and learning technology skills for academic staff, where gaps were reported across the sector. Finally, communication skills, sometimes related to customer service provision, were widely held to be in need of development.

In the light of this survey evidence, eight main workforce development priorities were identified. The first, essential to underpin future analyses of the sector's workforce, is the improvement of the definition, collection, reporting and dissemination of higher education labour market information. This has begun with further development and refinement of the HESA staff record, particularly to include all staff and permit some minimal career tracking across the sector. The proposed Lifelong Learning Sector Skills Council is expected to bring further resources and expertise to this area.[5]

Another priority was to continue to improve equal opportunities for all who work or seek to work in higher education. This has been addressed in part by the creation of the Equality Challenge Unit (ECU) in 2000. Severely under-resourced in its early years, the ECU has nevertheless been a very valuable addition to the sector, bringing specialist expertise and networks and providing back-up for institutions' own efforts in ensuring that good practice is identified and disseminated.

Lord Dearing's report on the higher education sector (NCIHE, 1997) gave considerable prominence to the need to encourage higher education staff to engage with professional development in learning and teaching and his recommendations led to the creation of the Institute for Learning and Teaching in Higher Education (ILTHE). The later sector workforce development survey went further and identified that engagement in professional development was particularly important for part-time and learning support staff. This critical area for higher education has now been given further impetus by the report of the sector's Teaching Quality Enhancement Committee (HEFCE et al., 2003) and the recent White Paper on higher education (DfES, 2003). The activities of both the ILTHE and the Learning and Teaching Support Network (LTSN) are set to be stimulated further by the creation of the proposed Higher Education Academy for the Enhancement of Teaching and Learning early in 2004. Both organizations complement extensive efforts within individual institutions and the LTSN's networking approach, which builds on already strong subject and discipline networks and communities of practice, working very much with the grain of academic life.

Meeting the training and career development needs of research staff effectively is a priority that was identified in the workforce development plan and which has been discussed more recently in successive studies and reports (HEFCE, 2003a, 2003b; HM Treasury, 2003). The White Paper (DfES, 2003) focuses on the theme in its recommendations for rewarding talented researchers and for rigorous new standards for government-funded research postgraduate places.

Perhaps the most potentially influential strand identified in the workforce development priorities, and one that is underpinned by considerable further research and development work by the sector's representative bodies and agencies (UUK, 2003), is the need to increase investment in leadership and management development and to devise a sector-wide strategy for leadership and senior management development in particular. This is now being taken forward in the proposals for a Higher Education Leadership Foundation, a new sector-owned and led body, which will receive significant financial support from the UK funding councils and is planned to be in operation by early 2004.

The aim of the Leadership Foundation (UUK, 2003) is to enhance the competitiveness, efficiency and effectiveness of UK higher education by further developing the professionalism and profile of leadership, management and governance in the sector. It will do this by addressing individual and institutional development, fulfilling foresight functions and acting as a champion and co-ordinator for the sector. It will be the strategic focus, central resource and co-ordinating point for leadership, management and governance development in higher education. It will broker international and cross-sector development opportunities, commission and design programmes and projects for its clients, undertake market research, identify and disseminate good practice and resources, assist institutions to develop their own capacity and lead the debate on enhancing individual and institutional performance.

A further area for priority attention is the establishment of a national framework for technical skills development and training in order to encourage trainee-entry recruitment, enable multi-skilling among experienced technicians, and provide more effective management of technicians. This is now being taken forward with the support of funding provided by the Sector Skills Development Agency (SSDA), building on preliminary work in a number of higher education institutions to identify and codify the relevant skills and competences needed by technical staff.

A theme that is familiar in all employment sectors is the need to address skills gaps in IT, and higher education is no exception. IT skills are being tackled in higher education through additional funding, awareness raising, training and networking initiatives led by the Joint Information Services Council (JISC).

Finally, but by no means the least important workforce development priority, is the historic lack of investment in basic and other skills training for the thousands of staff employed in higher education on manual grades – estimated at some 70,000 people (HESDA, 2002, 11). The growing number of active employee development schemes in higher education institutions is testimony to the importance being given to this area by the sector. The outcomes are contributing not only to the skills development of this large and vital part of the workforce but also, as is the case with all training and development, to the enhancement of quality in our institutions.

The proposed Lifelong Learning Sector Skills Council is expected to take forward this strategic agenda and to assume most of the core functions of a number of the former National Training Organisations, including HESDA in relation to the higher education sector. Its aim is to have in place by 2010 'an integrated framework of workforce standards and qualifications for the lifelong learning sector [in a context where] employers will be investing in workforce development at record levels' (ALP et al., 2003). At the time of writing it is expected that the former Information Services NTO (ISNTO) will be one of the initial partners in the Sector Skills Council, obviously bringing with it the particular perspective of library and other information staff.

The key role of leadership and management development

Leadership and management development and their strategic importance to the sector is emphasized above. The acknowledged need for significant investment – ideally within a strategic and co-ordinated framework – is not indicative of any crisis in the management of higher education, but rather reflects the recognition by higher education leaders and by higher education's many stakeholders that excellent management and leadership, at all levels in our institutions, are critical factors in assuring continuing success.

Commentators frequently emphasize *senior* or *strategic* leadership and management development and, indeed, this will be the primary focus of the Leadership Foundation. But it is vital not to lose sight of the fact that leadership and management roles exist in a university or college – as in any organization – at many different levels, and the development needs associated with the full range of management roles need to be addressed. HESDA and its predecessors have a long record of collaborating with the Society of College, National and University Libraries (SCONUL) and the Universities and Colleges Information Systems Association (UCISA) in development programmes for library and information staff holding senior strategic management positions, those in middle management roles and those in first line management positions.

Key institutional factors underpinning effective continuing professional development

A report published in 1994 (UCoSDA, 1994) identified a range of factors that lead to effective, strategic continuing professional development, which still hold true.

First and foremost, CPD, and the resources to support it, need to be planned strategically as an integral part of institutional planning processes at all levels. The increasing use in higher education of quality enhancement tools such as the Investors in People (IiP) Standard or the European Foundation for Quality Management Excellence Model has stimulated moves to integrate strategic staff development and training and such models are proving powerful catalysts to both organizational and individual development and performance, including the effective integration of staff appraisal and CPD provision.

Secondly, the active encouragement and endorsement of the value of engaging in CPD by senior leaders is essential and it follows from this that institution-wide co-ordination of all staff development and training needs to be afforded a legitimate strategic position in institutional structures. This means that the management roles and responsibilities for staff career and professional development need to be clearly defined and adequate training provided.

Library staff: generic and specialist challenges

Few of the national surveys quoted in this overview of the sector identify library staff as a discrete category of the workforce.[6] It is nevertheless clear that the generic issues facing higher education apply in equal measure to library staff. Like all staff groups they need to review and update definitions of profession-specific skills and maintain their professional competence; like all staff groups they are addressing generic staff development needs including particularly leadership and management, team working and customer service skills; and like all staff groups they are adapting to and exploiting more flexible working patterns arising from the increased diversity of the sector, as well as the inevitably competing requirements from generally more demanding customers.

But library staff are also at the forefront of the information revolution, the radical nature of which is clear from subsequent chapter headings. Changes in the way knowledge and information are being created, managed and used are altering and to some extent challenging the roles of library staff in our higher education institutions. In a recent conference paper Fisher (2002) reported on the results of a survey and analysis of the current and future skills and competences needed by information professionals. She identified six emerging areas for priority action: knowledge management, project management, user support, leadership, strategic thinking and ICT applications. A critical strategic issue for the sector is to ensure that employers, educators, professional bodies and individual professionals are moving in concert to address this enormous change to the lifeblood of higher education: information and knowledge.

Only with highly effective and visionary leadership and management will all our opportunities be grasped and exploited. Higher education needs leaders who can exploit the new opportunities by embracing change, motivating their colleagues and improving services for their increasingly diverse clientele. We need team players who welcome opportunities to work across conventional boundaries, creating new roles and integrating specialist services in a strategic framework designed to enhance further the quality and effectiveness of our higher education institutions. None of this will be achieved by chance. It must be planned and managed and, above all, staff development and training for all staff must be approached as an investment and not a cost.

Notes

1. The Higher Education Staff Development Agency (HESDA) is the lead agency for developing the skills, training and qualifications of people who work in higher education. Evolving out of the Universities Staff Development Unit (USDU) (1989–92) and the Universities and Colleges Staff Development Agency (UCoSDA) (1992–7), it is committed to promoting strategically planned staff development and training and related initiatives across the UK higher education sector. It was designated the National Training Organisation (NTO) for higher education in

1997 and led the development of the Sector Workforce Development Plan (SWDP) in partnership with sector stakeholders.

2. A Sector Workforce Development Plan (SWDP) is a strategic document describing the main skills development priorities for employers. SWDPs are prepared by NTOs for each employment sector in the economy and are intended to inform the development of national, regional and local skills development policies and initiatives.

3. HESDA's second Skills Foresight Report maps the higher education labour market, identifying trends where possible, with a particular focus on skills issues. It reviews evidence for the whole workforce, drawing on data from the Labour Force Survey (National Statistics Office, 2001), the IES/HESDA Higher Education Staff Development Agency (2001) employer survey (staff skills, training and development), and the Universities and Colleges Employers Association (2001) employer survey (staff recruitment and retention).

4. With approximately two-thirds of the higher education workforce made up of graduates, higher education institutions themselves educate and train most staff employed in higher education before and during employment. This is the case for academic and research staff and most professional, technical and other staff. As independent awarding bodies, higher education monitors and evaluates its own provision, underpinned by internal and external quality assurance systems. Most higher education institutions offer employees a wide range of accredited and non-accredited training opportunities through internal staff development units and departments. Additional training is provided by further education colleges and work-based training and assessment centres, and by professional bodies and trades unions.

5. Sector Skills Councils (SSCs) are being created to replace the network of National Training Organisations (NTOs), which has been in place since the mid-1990s. The new network of SSCs (supported by funding from an independent Sector Skills Development

Agency) is to consist of fewer, larger, more strategic bodies than the NTOs. The granting of a licence as an SSC will give groups of employers in sectors with an employment base of economic or strategic importance responsibility for providing influential leadership to strategic targeted action to meet their sector's skills, workforce development and business needs. In the field of lifelong learning six partners are collaborating to propose a Sector Skills Council that will include higher education. The six partners are the Association of Learning Providers (ALP), the Employment NTO (ENTO), the Further Education NTO (FENTO), HESDA, the Information Services NTO (ISNTO) and PAULO, the NTO for community-based learning and development.

6. The Labour Force Survey uses the Standard Occupational Classification (SOC) 2000 system to identify occupations occurring within higher education. The nine classes are (1) managers and senior officials; (2) professional occupations; (3) associate professional and technical occupations; (4) administrative and secretarial occupations; (5) skilled trade occupations; (6) personal service occupations; (7) sales and customer service occupations; (8) process, plant and machine operatives; (9) elementary occupations. Library staff are not separately identified but occur mainly in classes (2), (3) and (4).

References

Association of Learning Providers et al. (2003) *Position Paper on the Formation of a Lifelong Learning Sector Skills Council*, unpublished report to the Sector Skills Development Agency.

Department for Education and Skills (2003) *The Future of Higher Education*, Cm 5735, London, The Stationery Office.

Fisher, B. (2002) Skills for the Future Information Professional: the role of individuals, educators, professional bodies and employees. In Fraser, M. (ed.), *The Vital Link 3: staffing in library and information services in the 21st century. Proceedings of the third national staffing conference, 29–30 November 2002,* University of South Australia, Adelaide.

Higher Education Funding Council for England (2002) *Rewarding and Developing Staff in Higher Education: interim evaluation*, Bristol, HEFCE.

Higher Education Funding Council for England (2003a) *Joint Consultation on the Review of Research Assessment*, HEFCE 2003/22, Bristol, HEFCE.

Higher Education Funding Council for England (2003b) *Improving Standards in Postgraduate Research Degree Programmes*, HEFCE 2003/23, Bristol, HFCE.

Higher Education Funding Council for England et al. (2003) *Final Report of the Teaching Quality Enhancement Committee on the Future Needs and Support for Quality Enhancement of Learning and Teaching in Higher Education*, London, Universities UK.

Higher Education Staff Development Agency (2001) *Higher Education: sector workforce development plan*, Sheffield, HESDA.

Higher Education Staff Development Agency (2002) *Higher Education: the second skills foresight report*, Sheffield, HESDA.

Higher Education Statistics Agency (2002) *Resources of Higher Education Institutions 2000/01*, Cheltenham, HESA.

HM Treasury (2003) *Lambert Review of Business–University Collaboration: summary of consultation responses and emerging issues*, www.hm-treasury.gov.uk.

National Committee of Inquiry into Higher Education (1997) *Higher Education in the Learning Society*, chaired by Lord Dearing, London, HMSO.

National Statistics Office (2001) Labour Force Survey, (quarterly), NSO.

Office for Public Management (2002) *Development of Human Resource Strategies: learning from assessing strategies and advising institutions: a report to the HEFCE by the Office for Public Management*, Bristol, HEFCE.

Thewlis, M. (2001) *Recruitment and Retention of Staff in UK HE: a survey and case studies*, report commissioned by the HEFCE, SCOP, UCEA and UUK, London, IRS Research.

UCoSDA (1994) *Continuing Professional Development (CPD) for Staff in Higher Education (HE): informing strategic thinking*, Occasional Green Paper 10, Sheffield, UCoSDA.

Universities and Colleges Employers Association (2001) *Recruitment and Retention of Staff in UK Higher Education*, UCEA.

Universities UK (2003) Business Case for the Leadership Foundation for Higher Education, London, UUK.

Other sources consulted

Chambers, J. (2003) *Managing to Effect in Higher Education? Effective leadership and management in UK higher education academic units*, Discussion Paper Series 1, Sheffield, Higher Education Statistics Agency.

Deloitte & Touche (2002) *Rewarding and Developing Staff in HE: evaluation of phases 1 and 2, a report to the HEFCE by Deloitte and Touche*, Bristol, Higher Education Funding Council for England.

Gamble P. R. and Blackwell J. (2001) *Knowledge Management: a state of the art guide*, London, Kogan Page.

Higher Education Funding Council for England (2001) *Rewarding and Developing Staff in Higher Education*, Bristol, HEFCE.

Higher Education Funding Council for England (2002) *Rewarding and Developing Staff in HE: outcome of phase two, report on funded projects*, HEFCE 2002/45, Bristol, HEFCE.

Neocosmos, S., Thackwray, R. and Colling, C. (2003) *Rewarding and Developing Staff in Higher Education: a response to the development, impact and evaluation of the HEFCE Human Resource Strategy Initiative*, Briefing paper 109, Sheffield, Higher Education Staff Development Agency.

2

Rethinking professional competence for the networked environment

Sheila Corrall

Introduction

Advances in information and communication technologies are having a significant impact on library and information services in all sectors of society. Academic libraries have historically been at the forefront of electronic library developments and the use of information technology (IT) in the sector can be traced back over more than four decades, but there is no room for complacency as the changes currently in train are arguably more profound and more extensive than those experienced in previous eras. This chapter will look at the new electronic environment, the changing roles that it requires and the consequent implications for staff development.

The new electronic environment

In his turn-of-the-century overview of 40 years of libraries and IT in higher education, Cliff Lynch, Director of the USA-based Coalition for Networked Information, identifies three distinct phases of development, showing how the focus and nature of IT-related change in libraries has shifted over time, taking us from the modernization achieved through automation to the innovation and transformation driven by network technologies (Lynch, 2000).

From computerization to networking

In the first period of automation, libraries began to use IT to manage their (print-based) collections by computerizing routine 'housekeeping' operations, thus improving their efficiency. This period also included the introduction of shared catalogue records, which enabled a significant reduction of staff effort in that area. The second period was characterized by a step-change in user access to library catalogues and bibliographic information with the advent of online public access catalogues and direct end-user access to abstracting and indexing services via standalone and networked CD-ROM products. The latter offered end-users access to systems and facilities that were previously the specialist preserve of staff trained in online searching and signalled a transfer of activity from library staff to library users.

The third period represents the real beginning of the electronic library with the arrival of online content, initially in the form of CD-based and web-enabled access to the full text of journal articles, but also including the digitization of historic collections of archives, manuscripts and rare books. The rapid emergence of the world wide web as a universal channel for communication of information has complicated the picture with the huge quantity of dynamic information available online within and beyond higher education institutions, raising questions for academic libraries about the boundaries of their responsibilities. Many libraries are extending their remits to cover electronic delivery of institutionally generated information such as exam papers and research outputs and as a result are assuming new roles in digital asset management and becoming involved in scholarly communication and institutional publishing.

The distinguishing feature of the present era is the network dimension coupled with ubiquitous computing. Academic library users today expect easy, seamless access to information resources and services from anywhere in the world around the clock. Developments in computer-mediated communication have given rise to new concepts such as 'networked learner support' (Fowell and Levy, 1995; Bouchet, 1998) and, more specifically, 'networked reference assistance' and the virtual reference desk (VRD) movement, where libraries often work collaboratively with global partners (for example, via the *QuestionPoint* service developed by the Library of Congress and OCLC), but are also operating in competition with alternative information providers, notably Google Answers (Bakker, 2002; Kenney et al., 2003). These services use e-mail, web forms, conferencing systems, internet relay chat and other network technologies to provide either asynchronous or synchronous support to library users.

In previous eras libraries were often ahead of other parts of their institutions in electronic delivery, but now they are part of a much larger configuration of computer-based facilities and activities supported by local, regional, national and global networks. Library staff therefore now need to co-ordinate and, ideally, to integrate their systems and services with other campus provision to optimize efficiency and effectiveness. Until recently the main concern was to achieve interoperability between library management systems and institutional administrative databases for student records, personnel and finance, but the focus has now shifted to the integration of electronic library provision with systems supporting learning, teaching and research.

The learning information space

The use of IT in teaching and learning has evolved over the past decade from a pattern of uneven activity, largely dependent on individual initiatives of innovators and enthusiasts, to a position of mainstream provision, typically guided by institutional strategies for e-learning emerging as part of their learning and teaching and/or information (technology) strategies, often in the context of internationalization and the development of distance education programmes. The method of deployment has similarly evolved from fragmented application of presentation and communication technologies to their co-ordinated exploitation through integrated course management systems or virtual learning environments (VLEs). While some users, notably medical schools, have developed their own in-house learning management systems, most institutions are now purchasing site licences for off-the-shelf commercial products such as WebCT and BlackBoard. In many cases the level of engagement with e-learning across an institution varies significantly among departments even after adoption of a standard platform and this has led to the introduction of targets and incentives to achieve at least a basic online presence for all programmes of study.

In the UK, developments in this area have been given further impetus by programmes sponsored by the Higher Education Funding Councils and the Joint Information Systems Committee (JISC), such as the Computers in Teaching Initiative, the Teaching and Learning Technology Programme, the Exchange for Learning (X4L) Programme and Digital Libraries in the Classroom (the latter, significantly, a joint UK–USA venture, funded in conjunction with the National Science Foundation). In 2003, the Government's White Paper *The Future of Higher Education* promised that the Higher Education Funding Council for England would work with partners to 'embed e-learning in a full and sustainable way within the next ten years' (DfES, 2003a) and a later consultation document, *Towards a Unified e-Learning Strategy*, reinforced that commitment and flagged the need for inter-institutional and cross-sectoral collaboration to smooth links between universities, colleges and schools (DfES, 2003b).

VLEs generally provide facilities for individual and group communication (via e-mail, notice boards, conferences, chat rooms, and so on) as well as administrative and educational information (such as module descriptions, timetables, reading lists, lecture notes, assignments and quizzes). They allow tutors and students to upload documents to the course area and to link in resources from other websites. Most institutions now recognize the need to interface or integrate their VLEs with their student record systems to create a seamless managed learning environment (MLE) enabling automatic data transfer between the two systems, but the relationship between library management systems and VLEs and the position of libraries in MLEs are less well defined.

MLEs represent both an opportunity and a threat to academic information provision. Many academic libraries already provide electronic information resources through library websites and subject gateways, some also offer e-learning resources and web-based training materials for information skills development. Libraries have also been involved in developing electronic collections of core readings for students, notably via the UK Higher Education Resources On the Net (HERON) service, which clears copyright and digitizes book chapters and journal articles for e-reserve collections. However, with the advent of VLEs, academic staff are also becoming involved in information provision and often not communicating or consulting with library staff over resource selection and description. John MacColl (2001) identifies several problems and potential solutions arising from MLE developments, with reference to the JISC-funded ANGEL project, which aims to develop an Authenticated Networked Guided Environment for Learning. One concern here is the risk of a shift away from institution-wide provision (via the library) to course-restricted access (via the VLE) and another is the need to re-engineer traditional library acquisition and cataloguing procedures by introducing new online tools for the management of digital content.

Library staff need to aim for both service and systems integration in the new networked world and to grapple with complex interactions in the 'learning and information space' in the online environment. Neil McLean (2002) draws on the Australian Government-sponsored Collaborative Online Learning and Information Service (COLIS) project to identify the 'functional chunks' to be integrated, which include systems for library e-services, e-reserve and e-journals; content management; learning content management; learning management; digital rights management and directories services. McLean urges libraries to collaborate closely with other key learning and information stakeholders (academic and technical) in their institutions and to be prepared for a redefinition of boundaries between library and other domains. Areas where joint working is needed include the metadata infrastructure, rights management, portal developments and access (authentication and authorization) services.

The scholarly knowledge system

In research, IT has had a significant impact on the methods used and the subject matter investigated as well as on the whole scholarly communication system. Libraries have naturally played a part in the evolution of scholarly communication, gradually migrating their periodicals subscriptions from hard copy collections through parallel provision of print and digital resources to increasingly electronic-only access. Electronic provision has the potential to solve many of the problems associated with print journals, such as the difficulties of providing multi-user and multi-site access and the limitations of paper as a medium for representing some types of knowledge. However, while there have been significant gains from electronic publishing, the situation has become much more complex and challenging for both libraries and researchers, with renewable licences replacing outright purchases and other restrictions (such as IP-controlled access, high prices, bundled subscriptions and 'lock-in' agreements).

There have been various initiatives to deal with this situation, collectively referred to as the 'open access movement', which have pursued two complementary strategies of promoting alternative models of scholarly journals offered either at lower prices than commercial competitors or on a different basis (such as pay-to-publish rather than pay-to-access) and encouraging academic authors to deposit ('self-archive') their papers in institution-based or discipline-based open electronic archives or repositories. Proponents of open archives, such as Stevan Harnad (2001), have promoted the potential role of libraries in helping researchers to archive their work as 'e-prints' and maintaining institutional archives as 'an outgoing refereed collection for external use, in place of the old incoming collection via subscription costs for internal use'. Harnad also argues that library consortia can help journal publishers committed to change, as has been shown by the success of the Scholarly Publishing and Academic Resources Coalition (SPARC) formed by the USA Association of Research Libraries in 1998.

Peter Suber, author of the *Free Online Scholarship Newsletter*, suggests that librarians should deposit their own scholarly output in open access archives such as E-LIS (E-Prints in Library and Information Science) and DLIST (Digital Library of Information Science and Technology) (Suber, 2003). Academic libraries around the world are now actively engaged in setting up and running institutional repositories, with support in the UK provided through the JISC Focus on Access to Institutional Resources (FAIR) Programme. Although standards and tools continue to evolve, most commentators agree that the challenges here are not technical – or even financial – but essentially cultural, with differences between disciplines adding another dimension to the problems faced by library staff trying to populate repositories (Pinfield, 2003; Day, 2003).

Writing on the future of the university in the digital age, James Duderstadt (2000) of the University of Michigan notes that research and scholarship are already heavily dependent on computers, networks and digital libraries – for example, to simulate physical phenomena, to link investigators in virtual laboratories or 'collaboratories' and to provide scholars with access to knowledge resources. IT is not only enabling researchers to address previously unsolvable problems, it has actually created simulation as a third mode of research alongside theory and experimentation. Similarly, IT has encouraged the shift from solitary scholarship to collaborations of research teams spanning many disciplines, institutions and countries. Duderstadt sees the library of the future as a 'center for knowledge navigation, a facilitator of information retrieval and dissemination' but in a significantly different way, pointing to profound changes that will 'involve the evolution of software agents, collecting, organizing, relating, and summarizing knowledge on behalf of their human masters'.

The big IT-related development in research is 'e-science', the term commonly used to represent the increasingly global collaborations of researchers interacting with very large-scale shared resources supported by a sophisticated technology infrastructure, known as 'the Grid'. Such resources include massive distributed data collections and knowledge bases as well as high-performance computing, instrumentation, visualization and networking facilities. The new 'cyberinfrastructure' offers technical capacity and functional comprehensiveness of unprecedented depth and breadth and will transform the conduct of research, not only in science and engineering, but also in social sciences and humanities.

In the UK, the Labour Government has invested £120 million since 2000 through the research councils and the Department of Trade and Industry (DTI) to develop national e-science capacity. The DTI envisages the Grid as 'a flexible, secure and co-ordinated resource-sharing infrastructure, based on dynamic collections of computational capacity, data storage facilities, instruments and wide area networks which are as easy to access as electricity in the home' (DTI, n.d.). In the USA, the National Science Foundation has similarly set out its vision for an ambitious research programme, estimated to require $1 billion per year, emphasizing the potential for working across traditional boundaries, by enabling 'the federation of the necessary multidisciplinary, multi-institutional, and geographically dispersed human expertise, archival data, and computational models' (National Science Foundation, 2003). The UK Research Councils have also emphasised interdisciplinary work in this context.

The generation of enormous volumes of data by e-science experiments will move us beyond theory, experiment and 'in silico simulation' to a new era of collection-based research involving the systematic mining of very large datasets, where metadata standards, data federation, cross-collection tools and fusion services will be required. Tony Hey and Anne Trefethen, Director and Deputy Director of the UK e-Science Core Programme, argue the case for creating new types of digital libraries for scientific data with the same sorts of management services as digital libraries for conventional literature in addition to other data-specific services. Such services will thus not only include facilities for data manipulation, management, discovery and presentation, but will also provide tools for data curation, transformation, visualization and mining (Hey and Trefethen, 2002).

Hey and Trefethen also envisage a convergence of scientific data archives and text archives, whereby scientific papers routinely have active links to original data, other papers and electronic theses, so that researchers have seamless access to information and processing on demand from their bench, desktop or in the field. They see this as 'a large issue with profound implications for university libraries'. Technical interoperability of data archives and text repositories will therefore become an important concern for libraries alongside the interworking of library services and learning resources identified above. Hey and Trefethen see libraries as obvious organizations to take responsibility for hosting and curating (digitally) all the research papers produced by universities, but they leave open the question of responsibility for hosting and curating the scientific data produced by researchers, although they are clear that data curation and longer-term preservation require collaboration between all parts of the community, including scientists, librarians and IT specialists. Potential synergies between libraries and e-science are also flagged in the final report of the Research Support Libraries Group (2003) established by the UK funding councils.

A key point here is that while it is possible conceptually to separate research/e-science and learning/teaching and to identify distinct workflows for these academic processes, both sets of activities are ultimately dependent on the same original sources of data and information, which are continuously used, reused and repurposed to advance knowledge and understanding. Liz Lyon, Director of the UK Office for Library and Information Networking (UKOLN), uses the concept of a 'scholarly knowledge cycle' to elaborate these relationships and explains how the eBank UK project aims to improve the transparency of scholarly processes by addressing issues such as the provenance of digital resources and hierarchies of data and meta-data (Lyon, 2003).

Strategic alliances and partnerships

As already indicated, another defining characteristic of the current environment is collaborative working, both within and beyond the institution. Electronic information provision has required much closer collaboration between academic libraries and their computing and IT counterparts, and in many institutions has resulted in the unification of all information-related services into a large 'converged' information organization. Operational convergence through the physical collocation of library and other services to create 'one stop shops' for users is even more common than structural convergence, and it is generally the library building that is chosen to host an increasingly diverse range of resources and facilities, such as work-station clusters, training rooms, IT helpdesks, study skills centres, careers information points, video-conferencing suites and internet or learning cafés.

Libraries have a long history of inter-institutional collaboration, particularly for the electronic exchange and use of bibliographic data, evidenced by the development of publicly accessible union catalogues, such as COPAC (the online catalogue of the UK Consortium of University Research Libraries). However, technologies now available offer the opportunity for much deeper resource-sharing in a federated digital library enabling innovative local recombination, reshaping and reuse of collaboratively built, jointly owned, centrally pooled content (Seaman, 2003).

Another significant development is the shift towards library collaboration being institutionally determined (rather than library-led) with partnerships arising from strategic alliances formed at institutional level, including membership of regional, national and global university consortia, such as UK eUniversities Worldwide (UKeU), Universitas 21 and the Worldwide Universities Network (WUN).

Changing academic library roles

In the initial period of library automation the roles most affected were those of the clerical staff, typically library assistants, involved in handling book and borrower records for acquisition, cataloguing and circulation activities. The tasks of sorting, filing, counting and collating slips and forms were removed by computerization, and staff who took pride in their competence in carrying out such duties found their skills becoming redundant and their time being redistributed to areas where manual effort or a physical presence was still required (such as shelving books or staffing the counter). The introduction of shared or derived bibliographic data began to alter and routinize a lot of cataloguing work, which raised questions about the level of knowledge and skills needed to do the job. Meanwhile, the development of computer-based abstracting and indexing services created a new area of expertise in online database searching and many academic libraries established new specialist roles to exploit these facilities.

The Fielden Report on human resource management in UK academic libraries (John Fielden Consultancy, 1993) identified three groups of library staff whose roles were set to change most in the new universally networked environment – library assistants, subject or information librarians and senior managers. Fielden noted that paraprofessional and clerical staff were increasingly taking over cataloguing, classification and enquiry work from professionally qualified librarians and forecast this trend would continue to enable subject librarians to develop their role in academic support, while enhanced technological understanding, managerial skills and political acumen would be needed for the management of libraries, particularly for senior positions.

The emergence of paraprofessionals

Writing from a US perspective, Larry Oberg (1995) explains how automation of library processes and other factors resulted in a redistribution of workload with the creation of new tasks, realignment of old ones and – most significantly – emergence of a new category of staff, the paraprofessionals who 'administer major functional areas of our libraries, are assigned reference and information desk duties, perform a variety of systems work, and catalog most of the books added to our collections'. Thus paraprofessionals or 'support staff' now dominate functions such as acquisitions, cataloguing, document delivery and interlibrary loans, and in many libraries they have also assumed primary responsibility for basic reference services. Oberg envisages that eventually they will be given primary responsibility for the day-to-day running of academic libraries, but he also flags unresolved issues relating to pay, status and continuing education opportunities for this group of staff, whose success in their new roles will depend on fairer treatment and proper socialization into the professional values promulgated by librarians.

Mark Sandler (1996) similarly points to more diverse and higher level roles for library assistants in research libraries, resulting in blurred boundaries and functional overlap. His examples include reference work, systems development and maintenance, acquisitions and cataloguing (where the role of assistants has extended from downloading and upgrading bibliographic records to original cataloguing and subject analysis). Sandler also argues that advances in technology have created a new class divide among library workers leading to an 'ascendant class' of IT-savvy librarians and paraprofessionals while librarians possessing only supposedly simpler 'traditional' skills have suffered a loss of status. He predicts continuing transformation of the roles of professional and paraprofessional staff and a corresponding decline in the numbers of professionally qualified staff employed. Likewise, the Consortium for Educational Technology in University Systems (CETUS, 1997), formed by California State University and the City and State Universities of New York, envisages that paraprofessionals will increasingly assume supervisory and budgeting responsibility for units such as circulation, short loan or reserves and interlibrary loans.

The academic liaison librarian

The CETUS discussion paper sees librarians as 'indispensable counsellors in the electronic environment', working as advisers and teachers (rather than custodians of collections) and working with faculty and students in their own spaces (instead of only in the library building). Its key message is that the role of librarians is growing closer to that of teachers, becoming increasingly discipline-based and instructional or educational, including the following core activities:

- partnering with discipline faculty and other specialists for delivery of information and instruction
- designing instructional programmes for information access
- teaching students and faculty how to access information, whatever its format or location, and how to evaluate what they find
- serving as consultants on information resources, issues and problems
- developing and implementing information policy
- creating information access tools
- selecting, organizing and preserving information in all formats
- serving as leaders and facilitators in introducing information technologies and ensuring their effective use (CETUS, 1997, 5–6).

The bulk of this work will typically be the responsibility of staff variously described as 'subject', 'reference', 'liaison', 'information' or 'field' librarians. The term 'liaison librarian' or 'academic liaison librarian' has been chosen by many institutions to flag a shift in focus from looking after collections in a designated subject area to liaising with users from a named academic unit. Stephen Pinfield (2001) examines how this role has changed and developed in the electronic environment, drawing attention to increased emphasis on liaising ('connecting') with users and teaching information skills, on new approaches to (digital) reference and enquiry work and producing (web) subject guides, and on involvement with educational technology and project work.

Pinfield also stresses the importance of teamwork in this role, including working with library and computing colleagues. Kelsey Libner (2002) similarly emphasizes the need to collaborate with other players to create a coherent seamless information environment, suggesting a range of potential partners, such as information architects, instructional technologists, interface designers and computer scientists, as well as teachers and administrators. Libner envisages librarians 'using technology to guide online users to relevant databases, books, journals, and web sites . . . they will reduce the staggering complexity of a hybrid environment by presenting users with clear and useful choices among a few relevant options, regardless of their discipline, level of research experience, or means of access to the library'. Richard Biddiscombe (2002) sets out a bolder view of the subject librarian of the future, arguing that as 'learning support professionals' they have many of the skills needed to take on much of the generic tutorial and pastoral support currently provided by academic staff, which will have to be managed more efficiently with expected continuing pressure on resources.

The changing role of subject or liaison librarians shows how work in 'boundary-spanning' areas has become more complex as a result of technological developments. Collection development raises questions about including free resources (such as open-access journals) in OPACs or web pages and creating virtual collections by harvesting metadata from distributed repositories. User education has become more demanding with the multiple formats, huge volume and dubious quality of information available; expansion and diversification of the student population, with more mature, part-time, postgraduate, research and international students; integration of information skills with teaching, research and enterprise programmes; and high level concerns about copyright and plagiarism. Provision typically covers topics such as accessing electronic databases and journals; finding high quality resources on the web; keeping up to date with new information; using bibliographic software packages; carrying out citation and advanced database searches; and searching for systematic reviews. Delivery is usually tailored to the discipline, experience and priorities of students and staff and can take many forms, such as group sessions, individual support, self-paced learning packages (via the web or VLE) and team teaching with academic colleagues.

Strategic management of technology

The IT revolution has not only altered and developed established roles, it has also given rise to new specialisms and posts combining expertise in 'content' and 'conduit'. In many academic libraries, the traditional job of 'systems librarian', which was often located with bibliographic or technical services, has now evolved into a strategic role at senior management level, typically heading a team of specialists responsible for library systems, multimedia resources and web-related developments (Lavagnino, 1997). Titles such as head of systems or head of e-strategy are commonplace. New specialist posts are frequently offered as fixed-term appointments on the assumption that emerging areas require a focus of expertise initially until new practices become embedded. Examples include posts such as e-journals co-ordinator, metadata manager and online course librarian. Other new technical roles have emerged with externally funded digitization projects. The development of digital collections is also forcing librarians to rethink the cataloguing function to guard against establishing separate departments (and practices) for the description of manuscript, print and digital resources. The whole area of 'knowledge organization systems' is critical to the successful management and exploitation of the latter (Hodge, 2000).

Implications for staff development

It is widely acknowledged that the academic library world is already changing faster than it has ever done before and that the pace of change will continue to accelerate, with advances in information and communications technology being the key driver. Changes in the operating environment are being reflected in changes to staff roles, which in turn require the profession to rethink the skills, knowledge, understanding and motivation needed to design, develop and deliver a high quality professional service. Many organizations and individuals have investigated and commented on the skills needs of the library and information services workforce for the present and the future, with several large-scale studies being commissioned by the UK information services National Training Organisation (ISNTO, 2003, 2001; Skelton and Abell, 2001) and an in-depth study of senior management needs in academic information services funded by the Higher Education Funding Council for England (Dalton and Nankivell, 2002).

While these various studies differed in their purposes and scope, a common theme in all the reports is the increasing breadth and depth of the skillset (in its broadest sense) needed by library and information workers in the new electronic environment. Information-related skills are only part of a much larger picture of sector skills needs. The report by Val Skelton and Angela Abell (2001) on strategic information skills for the information services workforce in the knowledge economy usefully grouped the required knowledge, skills and attributes into three broad categories, which in turn can each be subdivided into two sub-categories as follows:

- professional and technical knowledge and skills
  - information (content) management competences
  - information technology (conduit) management competences
- business and management knowledge and skills
  - organizational (context-specific) competences
  - transferable (generic) competences
- individual and people skills and attributes
  - interpersonal (relationship) competences
  - personal (effectiveness) competences.

All the reports commented on the importance of IT skills and understanding for the information profession, but they all also ranked management and (inter)personal competences as the most critical and pressing development needs for the sector. In the current rapidly changing environment, academic library managers similarly must constantly pay attention to IT-related development needs, including needs arising from the impact of IT on information and content management, such as the introduction of new knowledge organization systems (metadata, ontologies, semantic networks, and so on) for digital resources. As in other sectors, 'business' (academic, education or research) knowledge, skills and understanding are essential to effective library performance and must be complemented by generic management and people competences for all staff.

Information and communication technologies

Most library collections will continue to combine traditional and digital resources for the foreseeable future, but library operations are already largely electronically based, both on the front line and in office and other work areas, with e-mail, local intranets and shared file stores underpinning much of the daily communication between staff. All library workers need to have at least the basic IT skills that enable them to use e-mail and the web. Manual, portering, reception and security staff must be included here to ensure that they are not cut off from communication channels. In addition, many libraries are broadening the roles of such staff to cover basic support for users, such as information about service availability and assistance with self-issue transactions.

Library assistants, paraprofessionals, technical teams, liaison librarians and others will all have particular IT-related knowledge and skills needs according to their roles, covering areas such as library, digital object and learning management systems. Staff providing access to e-journals need to be able to install and maintain all the plug-ins and add-ons now required to access primary and supplementary journal content. Diana Kichuk (2003) identifies eight different file formats for the former and many more for the latter. Staff involved in creating digital collections also need specialist knowledge and skills in areas such as mark-up languages and digital imaging (Hastings and Tennant, 1996).

However, there is a need to think beyond immediate job-related knowledge and skills needs. Technology is advancing so rapidly that what is learnt today will soon be superseded, so the requirement is really about developing the ability and willingness to learn new tools and techniques continually, rather than developing specific technical expertise. All library managers have a key role to play here in raising awareness among the whole library workforce about IT trends and issues in order to build understanding of the technical context for service and staff development. It is particularly important for senior managers to act as role models in developing their own understanding of the technical capacities of digital technologies and keeping their knowledge up to date, especially in relation to local and global developments in e-learning and e-science.

Academic integration and collaboration

The network is both the medium and the message of the new electronic environment. Learners, teachers and researchers want academic support services that are accessible and coherent, joined up with each other and to their own systems in a seamless whole. Library staff need to integrate their resources and services into managed environments for learning and research and they need to collaborate with others to achieve this goal. The key players here on the library side are the liaison librarians and senior managers who need to have the (human) networking, teamworking and other interpersonal skills to build collaborative relationships and work across academic and service boundaries. More critically, library staff need the capacity to relate, contextualize and extend their professional competence to fit the aims, programmes and cultures of all their partners. Patricia Battin (1998–2001) sees this ability as fundamental to our professional future: 'The one absolute and integrating requirement is to develop sufficient knowledge and understanding of each area of expertise outside of one's own in order to communicate and work productively with specialties other than one's own.' Computing or IT services are the most frequently mentioned service partners for libraries, but careers advisers are another group whose work needs to be co-ordinated with that of liaison librarians so that they can collaborate on embedding key skills development in the curriculum. Other partners for libraries include service departments and academic units at other institutions – often overseas – with whom their own institution has an alliance.

Battin also believes that in the new electronic environment there is a greater need for academic librarians to have in-depth knowledge of disciplinary specializations. This includes knowing what the discipline's primary questions are, how practitioners seek and use information, how the literature is structured and how patterns and methods of research and teaching are changing, especially in relation to use of digital technology. Pinfield (2001) confirms the advantage of librarians having a background in the subjects for which they are responsible, but accepts that a relevant first degree is not always essential, the crucial requirement being an appreciation of teaching and research techniques in the subjects, of the structure of the literature and of the key terminology and concepts. Many commentators stress the growing importance of teaching or instructional skills for subject and liaison librarians. Battin links the need for an 'ability to design and teach creative educational programs' with the advent of networks, the wide range of electronic resources and constantly changing literature structures. Biddiscombe (2002) goes further in arguing for 'a real and proven understanding of the learning process', evidenced by a formal pedagogic qualification (such as membership of the Institute for Learning and Teaching in Higher Education and/or completion of a recognized course in teaching and learning support). For both liaison librarians and library management, a broad and deep understanding of policy and strategy developments not only within their own institutions but also in the wider regional, national and international arenas is also essential for effective performance.

Managerial and personal competences

As Battin (1998–2001) reminds us, 'Librarianship at every level involves management of something – people, budgets, collections, projects, time, etc.; even … your boss!' and it has always done so. However, the new electronic environment, with its increased complexity and volatility, has introduced new management demands and involved more library staff in meeting these challenges. Paraprofessionals (as well as professionally qualified staff) often now need to develop competence in areas such as budgeting and recruitment and need to have the confidence to contribute to policy and planning (CETUS, 1997). Many digital library developments are financed through external project funding and this has put a premium not only on project management skills, but also on abilities in drafting project proposals, preparing grant applications and managing fund-raising activities (ISNTO, 2003; 2001).

Library staff in the networked world also need a wider set of personal skills and attributes to operate effectively. Examples include negotiating skills, to agree licensing terms and access rights for electronic resources; evaluation skills, to select high quality resources from the huge quantity available; and problem-solving skills, to respond quickly and flexibly to new and unexpected situations. The ISNTO (2003) Skills Foresight report notes a significant mismatch between the high priority given to problem-solving by employers and the low value assigned by practitioners. Battin actually puts such 'proficiencies' on a par with traditional skills: 'The abilities to learn quickly, to flourish in an ambiguous environment, and to design and execute creative solutions to new situations will be just as important as proficiency in the more traditional skills of cataloging, reference, and bibliography.'

Conclusion: rethinking staff development strategies

The success of the library of the future will be dependent on computer and human networks and the effective interworking of systems and people. Library staff roles are continually evolving and new information specialisms are arising frequently, often at the boundaries of existing professional groups. Academic library managers will need to deal with strategic issues surrounding the library's contribution to MLEs, institutional scholarly output, the management of scientific datasets and other concerns not yet identified.

Library staff development must evolve to meet these challenges. New competence frameworks are required to reflect the wider skills set, broader knowledge and deeper understanding needed at all levels, particularly in relation to IT, e-learning and e-science developments. Success will also depend on the possession of appropriate 'meta-competences' such as communication, self-development, creativity, analysis and problem-solving (Cheetham and Chivers, 1996). Staff development methods will similarly need to evolve to fit the new paradigm, with more emphasis on on-the-job and in-role approaches, including challenging assignments, project secondments, cross-functional teamwork and mentoring relationships. Liaison librarians and senior managers will benefit from engaging in action learning and research and other development activities alongside academic colleagues.

Academic library staff development planning and programming will therefore need to be managed strategically in collaboration with academic and service partners to match the new networked environment.

References

Bakker, T. (2002) Virtual Reference Services: connecting users with experts and supporting the development of skills, *LIBER Quarterly*, **12** (2/3), 124–37.

Battin, P. M. (1998–2001) Librarianship in the Twenty-First Century, *Syracuse University Library Associates Courier*, **XXXIII**, 43–61.

Biddiscombe, R. (2002) Learning Support Professionals: the changing role of subject specialists in UK academic libraries,

Program: electronic library and information systems, **36** (4), 228–35.

Bouchet, M.-L. (1998) Focus on the Internet: networked learner support, *INFOCUS*, **2** (3), www.lboro.ac.uk/departments/ls/cti/Networked.html.

Cheetham, G. and Chivers, G. (1996) Towards a Holistic Model of Professional Competence, *Journal of European Industrial Training*, **20** (5), 20–30.

Consortium for Educational Technology for University Systems (1997) *The Academic Library in the Information Age: changing roles*, Seal Beach, CA, California State University, www.cetus.org/acad_lib.pdf.

Dalton, P. and Nankivell, C. (2002) *Hybrid Information Management: skills for senior staff; final research report and recommendations*, Birmingham, University of Central England, www.himss.bham.ac.uk/researchdocuments.html.

Day, M. (2003) *Prospects for Institutional E-Print Repositories in the United Kingdom*, ePrints Supporting Study, 1, www.rdn.ac.uk/projects/eprints-uk/docs/studies/impact/.

Department for Education and Skills (2003a) *The Future of Higher Education*, Cm 5735, London, HMSO, www.dfes.gov.uk/highereducation/hestrategy/ pdfs/DfES-HigherEducation.pdf.

Department for Education and Skills (2003b) *Towards a Unified e-Learning Strategy*, Consultation Document, DfES/0424/2003, London, DfES, www.dfes.gov.uk/consultations2/16/.

Department of Trade and Industry (n.d.) *e-Science: building a global grid*, London, DTI.

Duderstadt, J. J. (2000) *The Future of the Research University in the Digital Age*, www.wiscape.wisc.edu/publications/evolutionrevolution.pdf.

Fowell, S. and Levy, P. (1995) Developing a New Professional Practice: a model for networked learner support in higher education, *Journal of Documentation*, **51** (3), 271–80.

Harnad, S. (2001) The Self-Archiving Initiative, *Nature*, **410**, 1024–5, http://cogprints.ecs.soton.ac.uk/archive/00001642/01/nature4.htm.

Hastings, K. and Tennant, R. (1996) How to Build a Digital Librarian, *D-Lib Magazine*, **2** (11), www.dlib.org/dlib/november96/ucb/11hastings.html.

Hey, T. and Trefethen, A. (2002) *The Data Deluge: an e-science perspective*, www.rcuk.ac.uk/escience/documents/DataDeluge.pdf.

Hodge, G. (2000) *Systems of Knowledge Organization for Digital Libraries: beyond traditional authority files*, Washington, DC, Council on Library and Information Resources, www.clir.org/pubs/reports/pub91/contents.html.

Information Services National Training Organisation (2001) *Skills Foresight in the Information Services Sector 2000–2007*, Bradford, ISNTO.

Information Services National Training Organisation (2003) *Skills Foresight in the Information Services Sector 2003–2009*, Bradford, ISNTO.

John Fielden Consultancy (1993) *Supporting Expansion: a report on human resource management in academic libraries, for the Joint Funding Councils' Libraries Review Group*, Bristol, Higher Education Funding Council for England.

Kenney, A. R. et al. (2003) Google Meets eBay: what academic librarians can learn from alternative information providers, *D-Lib Magazine*, **9** (6), www.dlib.org/dlib/june03/kenney/06kenney.html.

Kichuk, D. (2003) Electronic Journal Supplementary Content, Browser Plug-ins, and the Transformation of Reading, *Serials Review*, **29** (2), 103–16.

Lavagnino, M. B. (1997) Networking and the Role of the Academic Systems Librarian: an evolutionary perspective, *College & Research Libraries*, **58** (3), 217–31.

Libner, K. (2002) *Working the Network: a future for the academic library, paper submitted in response to the call for papers: Visions:*

the Academic 'Library' in 2012,
http://alpha.fdu.edu/~marcum/libner.doc.

Lynch, C. (2000) From Automation to Transformation: forty years of libraries and information technology in higher education, *EDUCAUSE Review*, **35** (1), 60–8,
www.educause.edu/pub/er/erm00/pp060068.pdf.

Lyon, L. (2003) eBank UK: building the links between research data, scholarly communication and learning, *Ariadne*, **36**, www.ariadne.ac.uk/issue36/lyon/.

MacColl, J. (2001) Virtuous Learning Environments: the library and the VLE, *Program*, **35** (3), 227–39.

McLean, N. (2002) *Libraries and e-Learning: organisational and technical interoperability*,
www.oclc.org/research/publications/archive/mclean_neil_20020
308_rev.doc.

National Science Foundation. Blue-Ribbon Advisory Panel on Cyberinfrastructure (2003) *Revolutionizing Science and Engineering through Cyberinfrastructure*, Arlington, VA, NSF, www.communitytechnology.org/nsf_ci_report/.

Oberg, L. R. (1995) *Library Support Staff in an Age of Change: utilization, role definition and status*, ERIC Digest, Syracuse, NY, ERIC Clearinghouse on Information and Technology, www.ericfacility.net/databases/ERIC_Digests/ed382197.html.

Pinfield, S. (2001) The Changing Role of Subject Librarians in Academic Libraries, *Journal of Librarianship and Information Science*, **33** (1), 32–8.

Pinfield, S. (2003) Open Archives and UK Institutions: an overview, *D-Lib Magazine*, **9** (3),
www.dlib.org/dlib/march03/pinfield/03pinfield.html.

Research Support Libraries Group (2003) *Final Report*, Bristol, Higher Education Funding Council for England,
www.rslg.ac.uk/.

Sandler, M. (1996) Transforming Library Staff Roles, *Library Issues*, **17** (1), www.libraryissues.com/sub/LI9609.asp.

Seaman, D. (2003) Deep Sharing: a case for the federated digital library, *EDUCAUSE Review*, **38** (4), 10–11, www.educause.edu/ir/library/pdf/erm0348.pdf.

Skelton, V. and Abell, A. (2001) *Developing Skills for the Information Services Workforce in the Knowledge Economy: a report on the outcomes of eight scenario planning workshops*, Library and Information Commission Research Report 122, London, TFPL.

Suber, P. (2003) Removing Barriers to Research: an introduction to open access for librarians, *College & Research Libraries News*, **64** (2), 92–4, 113, www.earlham.edu/~peters/writing/acrl.htm.

Other sources consulted

Case, M. M. (2002) Igniting Change in Scholarly Communication: SPARC, its past, present, and future. In Lynden, F. C. (ed.), *Advances in Librarianship*, **26**, San Diego, CA, Academic Press, 1–28, www.arl.org/sparc/SPARC_Advances.pdf.

3

Developing the academic library managers of the future

Patrick Noon

Introduction

The first part of this chapter will look briefly at the future for academic libraries in the UK, give detailed consideration to the resulting skill needs of future service heads, drawing especially on the work of the Hybrid Information Skills for Senior Staff (HIMSS) project, and suggest six core skill areas for future senior managers. The next section looks at the skills gaps and barriers to succession identified by current second-tier managers. The last section considers the need for proactive succession planning and approaches to skill development to address these gaps and barriers and challenges current library directors and second-tier staff to adopt them.

The Dilbert Principle

While those of us who work in higher education management continue with the comforting self-delusion that what we do has some value for the organization, it is sobering to remind ourselves that not everyone views management as positively as this. Scott Adams, in his entertaining cartoons and books on life among the managed (1997), acknowledges that he uses a lot of 'bad boss' themes in his work and that he will never run out of material as he receives hundreds of messages a day complaining about 'clueless' managers. Top of the list in his survey of the things that most annoyed staff about management was 'idiots promoted to management'. In the past this concept was known as the Peter Principle by which capable workers were promoted until they reached their level of incompetence. At least, suggests Adams, this principle generated managers who had once been good at something and held out the prospect for everyone to rise to a level of highly paid and comfortable incompetence. Now, Adams argues, the Peter Principle has been replaced by what he has christened the Dilbert Principle where 'the incompetent workers are promoted directly to management without ever passing through the temporary competence stage ... the most ineffective workers are systematically moved to the place where they can do least damage ... management'.

Reading some of the real life examples from Adams's books it is clear that the challenge to academic library managers is to change the way others see us. One way to do this is to ensure that we get the right people doing the right jobs as managers to guide us in the future. This is as true of academic libraries and information services as of anywhere else.

Mapping the future

A useful starting point for identifying how we develop information services managers for the future ought perhaps to be a look at what the future might be. Two places to start could be the vision of the Society of College, National and University Libraries (SCONUL) (2002) and the more detailed, if more eclectic, report for the Information Services National Training Organisation (ISNTO) by TFPL (2001), *Scenarios for the Knowledge Economy: strategic information skills*.

The SCONUL Vision predicts that, while the library will retain its importance in higher education organizations, the boundaries between functions will become increasingly fluid causing changes to staff roles. The information environment will become hybrid and the operating environment will continue to be complex. Services to users will be characterized by increasing diversity and there will need to be a willingness to adapt and meet these opportunities. The workforce will need to be more flexible to meet the challenges of the future including the blurring of roles between academic and support staff.

The ISNTO/TFPL report was far more wide-ranging and, therefore, more difficult to apply to the narrower perspective of higher education. It does, however, suggest that organizations will become increasingly dependent on their ability to manage knowledge and that information services will therefore assume a far more important role as strategies for knowledge and information become more highly developed and increasingly important to the organization. It also suggests that the role will become more multidisciplinary, attracting people with a diverse range of skills and experience. In a brief section on higher education, the report suggests that core organizational structures are unlikely to change in the short to medium term but that there will be a growing interest in knowledge flows and that information services should be taking a leading role in this. In general, there will be an increasing blurring of boundaries between formerly discrete areas of activity. The authors also offer strong support for research suggesting that successful organizations of the future will be built around the core competences of the organization rather than around its products or services.

There is a remarkable level of commonality between these visions of the future in which diversity, blurring of roles and boundaries, and an increasing complexity and dynamism in the environments in which libraries work are all common themes. However, there is not very much about how to manage these futures. Given that the changes posed are not particularly radical, it is tempting to think that there is an inbuilt assumption that management is taken as a generic element in any potential future; that management roles and the corresponding skills are unlikely to change quite as much as some of the more imaginative, if less than elegant, roles identified in the

ISNTO/TFPL report : chief surfer, futurist in chief and knowledge harvester are some particularly fascinating examples. The report does, however, acknowledge that strong leadership will be important in helping organizations chart their way through whatever the future holds. At the same time, it is one of the truisms of management theory that in uncertain and dynamic environments effective management is essential. It seems that some skills at senior level will still be just as important in the future as now and in the past, and so, by extrapolation, will be our need to ensure that we are able to provide people with the skills and experience to take advantage of future opportunities for the information services sector.

Mapping the skills

Another starting point for this chapter should be to try and develop some idea of what exactly it is that people in these senior management positions are expected to do.

HIMSS Project

One of the more extensive recent attempts to map the skills that may be needed for the future of information services in higher education was the Hybrid Information Skills for Senior Staff Project (HIMSS) (Dalton and Nankivell, 2002). Funded under the HEFCE Good Management Practice initiative, the purpose of the project was 'to contribute to the HE sector's succession planning for information management staff through the management development of "high-fliers"'. The project set out to identify the information management skills needed by senior managers of library, information and computing functions and then to see how this skills need could be translated into a coherent modular programme of management development. The project had a particular focus on what it called hybrid information skills – skills that could be applied across the very wide range of disciplines within larger converged information services. It hoped to identify any skills gaps in the current generation of managers working at 'deputy' level and how this gap might be bridged most effectively. The development of a self-diagnostic tool to enable managers to identify and address their own skills gaps was to be one of the ambitious deliverables from the project. Others included a detailed analysis of the skills set needed by senior managers and an evaluation of how this might be turned into a coherent pedagogical development framework for managers.

In developing the skills set, the project hoped to bring together a number of different perspectives. As well as asking senior managers in the sector and those aspiring to those roles, they also hoped to cross reference this with the views of directors of personnel in HE and with senior institutional personnel, typically pro-vice-chancellors, registrars or, if possible, vice-chancellors. Those with line management responsibility for information services were also interviewed.

One of the earliest, and certainly most valuable, parts of the project was the involvement of a number of directors of Information Services and university librarians in a workshop to help shape the research phase of the project by offering their views on the skills needed to undertake their roles successfully, on the critical skills gaps among aspiring directors and on the obstacles preventing these gaps from being closed. The outcome from the workshop was an initial list of the most frequently cited management skills needed to succeed at director level. These were:

- human resource management
- strategic management and vision
- financial management
- communication and interpersonal skills
- change management
- leadership skills
- negotiation skills.

When asked to identify the most common gaps among those aspiring to posts where these skills would be needed, the list included gaps in all the skills cited. There was one significant addition, however, which was what were called technical skills. These were defined as technical or professional skills gained as a direct result of working for some time in either libraries or information services and developing a close understanding of their culture.

None of the outcomes of this survey were particularly unusual or unexpected but what it did do, for perhaps the first time, was to produce some sort of consensus among senior managers of HE information services about what it is that we as a sector think are the skills needed for the effective management and delivery of services. Helpful as all of this is, it does not necessarily show whether these really are relevant skills for successful management in this kind of activity. The danger of asking current incumbents is that their answers will reflect their own background, culture and preoccupations and be potentially entirely self-referential. This was why other stakeholders were also asked for their views.

An important focus of the HIMSS Project was the views of aspiring managers. It is one thing for senior managers to identify skills gaps in their potential successors but quite another to learn of those gaps from the aspirants themselves. In the HIMSS Survey, the consultants had worked on the initial list of skills required for senior roles, grouping 19 of them under five broad headings:

- managing activities – including managing strategy and change and service delivery
- managing resources – including budget management and income generation
- managing people – including developing teams and performance management
- managing information – including decision-making and information systems
- managing projects – from inception to completion.

Against each of these skills respondents were asked to measure how important they thought they were for working as the head of an information service. In four areas the skills were all considered important for the role of head of service producing some valuable validation of the views of the present incumbents. The one area that was considered to be some way behind and considerably less important at the most senior level was project management, which had not appeared in the original list from existing heads.

While this may not be a scientific or definitive statement of the skills that need to be developed in the next generation of leaders, there is sufficient commonality across the groups to suggest that this is as good a list as we are likely to get from higher education. This is reinforced by the views of directors of personnel who were also asked what skills they were looking for in their heads of Information Services. They listed delivering a vision, planning strategically, and leadership and communication skills, all of which are entirely consistent with the views expressed by the heads and aspiring heads themselves.

Comparisons with skills from other sectors

To be certain that the skills are relevant it might be as well to look beyond our own insular concerns within the academic sector, and possibly outside libraries as well, as there are other sectors that are just as concerned about the development of the next generation of managers.

As well as *Scenarios for the Knowledge Economy*, published with TFPL, ISNTO has also conducted a Skills Foresight project for the information services profession (ISNTO, 2003), which includes libraries from all sectors in the UK. The 2003–9 report lists a number of management skills on which the profession continues to be reliant according to managers within the sector. Among the most important skills identified in the project are:

- risk management
- project management
- people management
- financial management
- change management

- strategic planning
- entrepreneurship and innovation
- leadership
- communication.

This is useful corroboration of the HIMMS skills checklist as it draws on a spectrum of libraries of which higher education is only one. It is still, however, based only on libraries. Another useful source of potential management skills to compare with these two from the libraries sector is the Civil Service's comprehensive senior management training programme from the Centre for Management and Policy Studies, which includes the Civil Service College (CMPS, 2001). The prospectus for their top management programme and the modular senior management programme 'Ten' offers modules covering:

- strategic vision
- characteristics of leaders
- skills to build and lead teams
- skills to increase personal effectiveness through self-knowledge
- skills to shape and manage change within complex organizations
- communication
- influencing skills
- sharing knowledge and skills experiences
- performance management
- problem solving

and, finally, that most rarely recognized skill, standing back and reflecting!

It is possible to go on looking at different lists of skills like this indefinitely but from the examples that we have explored so far it is possible to see not only a rich array of the kinds of skills that we should be developing in our managers of the future but also a strong correlation around some key or core skills common to all of these sources.

Skills in the following areas feature in every list in one form or another:

- managing change
- leadership
- strategic planning
- communication
- managing people
- financial management.

They presumably represent a reasonably well grounded core of skills around which our future managers could be developed. But it must not be seen as an exhaustive list because some of the ideas from other sectors, particularly the Civil Service, are intriguing and, if we are to believe regular comments from current heads, still important. Standing back and reflecting, creativity and entrepreneurship are a few skills that might not make a core list but would find their champions in many other surveys of management skills.

The skills gap

Having established a list of core skills, with several others on the fringe, we are led inevitably to the question of how well we have been developing those skills. If our aspiring heads of service are confident that they already have the skills to succeed to these posts, then as a sector we shall have done well in ensuring the future health of our services. If not, then we have a problem to address. What makes the second part of the HIMSS survey so interesting is that this is exactly the question that aspiring heads were asked: to assess their own skill level for each skill that they had identified as important in their future roles.

The results were extremely revealing. Those aspiring to move to heads of service roles as their next post agreed with the current heads that there was a considerable gap in the skills in which they felt fully competent and that they considered necessary to enable them

to fulfil those roles successfully. There was a particular lack of confidence in the areas of establishing strategies (16% felt they were fully
competent), analysing the external and internal environments (barely
20% felt fully competent), income generation (20% felt fully competent) and dealing with the poor performance aspect of people
management (24% felt fully competent). Lack of financial management and political skills, and even a lack of charisma and vision, were
quoted as potential barriers to promotion to head of service. There
were only a very few areas in which even half of the respondents felt
fully competent.

Of course, we have to be careful with this analysis. Respondents to
the survey are unlikely to think they are fully competent in all of the
skills they need to be a head of service partly out of natural self-
effacement and partly because they have only an imperfect idea of what
level of skills is actually needed, as distinct from that which they
assume is needed as an observer. Despite this, the survey suggests that
there is still much work to be done in ensuring that we have fulfilled
our obligations to secure some measure of effective succession planning. This view is reinforced by the finding in the ISNTO Skills
Foresight survey that although managerial skills were present in the
existing workforce, this was only the case in less than half of the
respondents. This implies that staff need training in these skills.
There was, however, an alarming decline – 4% decrease between
2000 and 2003 – in the number of libraries that intended to use training to address skills gaps, including the lack of management skills in
their organizations (ISNTO, 2003). Why is this and what are the other
barriers that are getting in the way of our aspiring heads acquiring the
skills that would make them confident to succeed to senior posts?

Barriers to succeeding to senior posts

Important as it is, this very significant skills gap was not the only difficulty faced by the aspiring managers studied in the HIMSS Project.
One of the most interesting parts of the Project explores the barriers
to progress to senior posts. For current heads of service, the chief obsta-

cles cited as reasons for failing to address these skills gaps effectively were:

- the culture of the organization and the service
- lack of support and or commitment at institutional level
- limited options for relevant training
- time and resources
- constant change.

This is an interesting list, as it appears to imply that the barriers to succeeding to senior posts are all created by the organization or by external forces, and that existing managers are simply passive agents in the process of developing skills in the managers of the future. Once again, it is even more interesting to compare this with the perceptions of the aspiring heads themselves.

Aspiring heads also identified a number of financial barriers, including rigid pay structures or inadequate salary levels, making it difficult to appoint people of the right calibre; but they also pointed to the decline in the number of senior posts that were available caused by institutional reorganizations such as convergence, leading to greater competition for fewer posts. There was a clear increase in the attention given to the location of posts and its impact on personal circumstances. This reduced mobility in the workforce was becoming another barrier to progress.

Two particular barriers were identified in managing converged services. The first was a concern over skills and experience. Some aspirants felt that they lacked sufficient experience in libraries or IT depending on which background they came from. The insistence on the right technical background for senior managers was also perceived as preventing the appointment of perfectly good candidates with good management experience. The second problem was that the potential attractiveness of an enhanced strategic role across a wider service was offset by concerns over dilution of the manager's own specialism in libraries or IT and a corresponding loss of credibility among peers in that specialism.

The final barrier is perhaps the most important of all. The HIMSS report was clear that the sector was very poor at succession planning, one of the most obvious ways to ensure a source of properly skilled and experienced candidates for the most senior jobs in academic libraries and information services. The survey report noted, however, that less than a quarter of the respondents were aware of any activities within their own organization or the sector generally that could be called succession planning, and less than 20% had had any direct involvement with such activities. These included management development programmes run by SCONUL, UCISA and HESDA; other generic management courses; appraisal schemes; peer group meetings; and regular or frequent acting up for senior managers. The report concluded, however: 'there is no formal succession planning for managers in information services in UK universities.'

Developing skills for the future

Succession planning

If we are to be serious about sustaining the best leadership of our libraries and information services some time and effort must be invested in exploring and overcoming some of these barriers to succeeding to senior posts and not believing that the solutions all rest with someone or something else. There is not much one can do to improve a person's charisma. It is difficult to think what a suitable training programme would look like, and it is possible that the issue of financial reward is symptomatic of higher education and there is little we can do to change it. But there ought to be ways of addressing many of the other barriers discussed above. A start would be to adopt a less dogmatic attitude to expecting new heads to have 'the right kind of experience' in libraries, IT or both, depending on the structure of our services. Given time and appropriate development, mentoring, support or patience, managers with different backgrounds could perform with great distinction, provided that they start with the right set of generic skills and personal qualities. There probably isn't much to be done about the decline in workforce mobility, but it is worth remembering that most of the library staff of the future are already in post. This obviously has enormous implications for succession planning within all institutions across the sector and is surely a barrier about which something can be done by all heads of service.

It is critically important to recognize that developing managers of the future takes time. To ensure a continuing supply of candidates able and willing to assume senior leadership roles, it is vital to make sure that they are already equipped with many, if not all, of the skills, experience and personal attributes that they will need long before they find themselves in those senior positions.

One of the most interesting things about the original course for aspiring university librarians, the SCONUL/HESDA Managing for Strategic Change Programme, happened when it was first broadened to include the Universities and Colleges Information Systems Association (UCISA). There was an immediate demand for the course from Computing and Information Services directors already in post who felt that they had missed out on the development of these skills. Once expanded in this way, it also began to interest some library directors for the same reason. Given the pressure under which many senior staff in higher education now work, this is no place to be learning on the job or making it up 'on the hoof'. The sector should be trying to find ways to ensure that there is a significant underpinning of skills and experience already in place to provide senior staff with the confidence to apply for, and meet the challenges of, these posts.

This does not just mean making sure that deputies, or other senior staff of equivalent rank, must always succeed to the head of service post. The greatest danger of shortsighted succession planning is that is deteriorates into the managerial equivalent of generations of inbreeding. Heads of service develop and select people who closely resemble themselves as a kind of, often unconscious, validation of their own abilities and professional credibility. On the contrary, the real requirement is to design successors in the best interests of the organization. The nature of the leaders of tomorrow ought to depend on a vision of what is to be achieved by libraries and information services in the future, not on reinforcing the past.

Starting from some form of consensus about the skills and personal attributes that can best deliver this vision is vital. This was why the Managing for Strategic Change course was built on generic, strategic management skills and avoided concentrating too much on a specific library or information sector context. Sadly, one of the criticisms of the programme, particularly from the IT participants, was that there was not enough of this contextualization and that it should be included to encourage IT directors to participate. This is potentially a retrograde step back to the kinds of programmes where experienced managers passed on the wisdom of what they had done over the years to succeed as managers, without providing any broader manage-ment skills framework on which delegates could fall back at their workplaces when the problems turned out to have a different shape from those that they had heard about from practitioners. In other words it was the wrong kind of succession planning. There is a place for the practitioner dimension but it ought to be only one small part of this development process, which should also offer a toolkit to apply to changing situations rather than provide ready-made answers to static problems. It is a lesson we seem curiously slow to learn.

Proactive skills development

Something else heads of service could do is to make a conscious effort to avoid 'deputy' level posts becoming too narrow in scope or too oper-ationally focused, so that incumbents can find the time within the scope of their role to develop the skills appropriate for the most senior posts as they progress, rather than having to make a quantum leap in order to succeed to those posts or trying to catch up once they have done so. This is more than just sending post-holders on appro-priate management courses. It could include heads adopting mentoring or coaching approaches, which provide a proper frame-work and structures within which those with the ability, and the inclination, can be helped to develop not just the skills but the experience, knowledge and political awareness that can often be gained on the job or passed on from the 'walking wounded' in post who have learned from their own experience. This is a proper way to use that experience.

Of course there is training and development either within our own organizations or across the sector. Beyond formal management qualifications and one-off training courses, there has not always appeared to be a great deal of management development activity aimed at generating the body of knowledge and skills to prepare leaders in our sector. It was this view that led to the development of a suite of management programmes between SCONUL, UCISA and HESDA, starting with an Introduction to Management course, which was, as its name implied, for those just moving into a management role; a course entitled Making Management Work, aimed at developing and improving the skills of those who had been managers for some time; and finally Managing for Strategic Change, aimed at those in or aspiring to the leadership roles in the sector.

Most of this training has been very successful. The introductory course is popular and continues to run twice a year, and Making Management Work, after a shaky start, has now developed a clear market. The strategic management course produced three very successful cohorts, and was soon remodelled to accommodate current heads as well as aspiring managers, who for all their experience and ability were aware of their own lack of formal skills development. This is a very good example of practitioners in the sector identifying a gap in the provision of management skills training and development and taking positive, and largely successful, action to deal with that gap. If there are no suitable existing programmes to help secure the effective management of the future, it is quite possible for those working in the sector to consider developing them, provided they have the commitment.

Quite apart from this, there are the academic management courses. The MBA remains the blue riband of management courses, but this is by no means the only course that improves management skills. There are others including masters degrees in Public Administration, and in Higher Education Management, and there is a wide range of diploma and certificate courses, not to mention a growing number of courses that build on experiential learning and work-based learning. These will not be for everyone, and you can almost hear the cries of 'too expensive', 'can't afford the time' or 'not geared to our needs', but the growing number of personal testimonies to the benefits that these programmes can bring suggests that providing an academic and theoretical framework within which to apply practical skills has something to offer to those who feel that this approach would suit them. These kinds of programmes produce successful managers in many other sectors, and they certainly should be seen as a means of developing skills for our future managers. As a sector, we should do more to explore, evaluate and promote these kinds of approaches.

Competences – an alternative approach

Skills appear to be only one part of the package that we need in our senior managers of the future. We also need them to exhibit the right kind of personal qualities to succeed. The HIMSS Project identified some of these personal qualities as well as the set of desirable core skills. These included leadership, which may be a skill as well as a personal quality, confidence, decisiveness and assertiveness, the ability to identify opportunities and develop partnerships, the ability to delegate, creativity (especially in times of constrained resources), entrepreneurship and the ability to innovate. This takes us a lot closer to the competences approach to management as distinct from the skills-driven approach that we have concentrated on so far. It would not be appropriate to leave this exploration of how we develop managers for the future without mentioning the competences approach, albeit briefly. Although comparatively recent in conception, the competences approach is increasingly popular in the private sector where there is a growing belief that it is the ability to develop and retain the right kinds of competences and capabilities that will offer a competitive edge for organizations. It has led to the concept of the 'learning organization', which puts this kind of development at the heart of its activities. It is curious that this concept has been so slow to gain recognition in higher education, at least at management level, although interestingly the ISNTO/TFPL report makes a point of highlighting this as a potentially important area for future development.

There are plenty of definitions and enough material to devote a chapter on its own to this approach but, in brief, competences focus on personal qualities such as behaviour, ability and attitude, rather than on responsibilities and tasks. They are about how people manage, and the outputs that they achieve, rather than on what they do and what knowledge they bring to the job. At other levels of activity and in other contexts there has been much interest in competences in the form of the growth of NVQ qualifications, but although this extends to management level there does not appear to be a lot of evidence of its acceptance as a measure of management ability, and certainly not in higher education.

The Management Charter Initiative

The Management Charter Initiative has tried to promote excellence in management for the best part of two decades now. It developed a set of management competences and the Chartered Management Institute has worked with the National Council for Vocational Qualifications (NCVQ) to develop these into three levels of management standards, including a Level 5 for senior managers. Level 5 offers options in operational and strategic management, and these offer another starting point for identifying how to ensure that we have the best managers for the future (CMI, n.d.).

Level 5 in strategic management assesses abilities in competences such as acting strategically, communicating, influencing others, and thinking and taking decisions, while the operational framework includes competences such as building teams and focusing on results. These are not in themselves very different from the skills set identified earlier. What is different is how the competences are expressed, demonstrated and assessed. In demonstrating competences in communication, for example, managers must show that they adopt communication styles appropriate to listeners, and show that they act strategically by clearly relating goals and actions to the strategic aims of the organization in which they work. In other words, there is far more focus on the outputs that the competences deliver than on the simple acquisition of skills. Another important difference is that the competences can be demonstrated from existing and previous work experience. This is of particular interest to those who have been in management for some time and want to demonstrate that, although they have few formal qualifications, they have been acting, and are perfectly capable of acting, at say a strategic level. It also ought to be of use for organizations as an audit tool to assess capabilities and potential, and as a cost-effective, work-based approach to developing managers to succeed to senior roles in the future.

This approach is not without its critics. There are plenty who argue that not only are the competences too difficult to define, but that the standards in which they are expressed are going to be either so accessible that everyone achieves them or so difficult that no one can. At the same time, there is the question of how to train or develop people to acquire these very personal qualities and attributes. There is insufficient space in this chapter to explore this in more detail but it should be recognized that this is an important approach, which offers us a great deal more than simply ticking the boxes as staff go on approved skills development courses. We should consider the competences approach seriously if we really want to be sure we are developing effective managers for the future.

Conclusion

Such visions as we have for the future suggest that librarians and information services will continue to be important to our organizations, but that the diversity of our roles, the fluidity of barriers between roles and the uncertainty of the future will all pose challenges to those who will manage those services. It is for others to judge whether past and present generations of senior managers have displayed and used effectively an appropriate array of skills and personal qualities, but it is clear that this generation has an important role in ensuring that the right kinds of skills and abilities are available for the next generation. The HIMMS Project has gone a great deal of the way to identifying exactly what they are. More than this, it has shown where current skills gaps exist, and some of the important barriers that are likely to prevent the next generation of heads of service succeeding to those roles. With such a wealth of information, and the long held commitment to skills development in information services, as well as the added value or alternative of the competences approach, it ought to be possible to fashion some framework that will enable us to be sure that the managers of the future succeed, not by good fortune, but by effective succession planning and sound foresight.

References

Adams, S. (1997) *The Dilbert Principle*, London, Boxtree.

Centre for Management and Policy Studies (2001) *CMPS Portfolio 2001–2*, London, CMPS.

Chartered Management Institute, www.managers.org.uk/institute/. Provides details of qualifications and curricula for NVQ accredited management programmes.

Dalton, P. and Nankivell, C. (2002) *Hybrid Information Management Skills for Senior Staff (HIMMS) Project*, Birmingham, University of Central England, www.himss.bham.ac.uk/. The site contains details of all of the research reports and the final research report from which data for this chapter has been collated.

Information Services National Training Organisation (2003) *Skills Foresight in the Information Services Sector 2003–2009*, Bradford, ISNTO.

Society of College, National and University Libraries (2002) *The SCONUL Vision*, London, SCONUL.

TFPL (2001) *Scenarios for the Knowledge Economy: strategic information skills*, London, TFPL.

4

Converging on staff development

Biddy Fisher

It is all too easy and too tempting to train people beautifully for yesterday's work and to pay too little heed to creating the work of the future (Handy, 1998).

Introduction

This chapter deals with the staff development issues that arise from converging libraries with other generic support departments. It traces briefly the history of convergence of library, computing and media services in the UK over the past decade and describes the more recent configurations that bring libraries together with education development departments. The implications for staff development are illustrated with examples taken from universities and colleges that have taken positive action to ensure that staff develop appropriate skills to deal with emerging learning environments. Scenarios for the future are outlined for readers to consider, and models of good practice in developing staff within converged services are offered.

Little progress has been made to challenge Mel Collier's assertion (1996) that no common understanding of convergence exists. Writing after many other authors had aired their views on convergence (see references for general reading at the end of this chapter), he traces the history of convergence from its UK beginnings in the late 1980s over an eight-year period. Outlining the major ways in which convergence arises, Collier cites managerial, service accretion or structural convergence as the most common. Subsequent evaluation of convergence was scarce, but this lack has not impeded the emergence of variations and other forms of convergence. Such was the power of the convergence message that the report by John Fielden Consultancy (1993), on the staffing issues arising from the Follett Report (Joint Funding Councils' Libraries Review Group, 1993), dedicated two pages to an analysis of convergence. The staffing and staff development implications, particularly of operational convergence, were recognized in this report.

From 1995 a different configuration began to appear, one that, arguably, creates a more significant opportunity for making a real change to the student (and academic staff) experience of a learning environment. Departments concerned with pedagogic development are now commonly found within 'learning centres' and are creating exciting opportunities for their staff. Such developments bring with them the exacting requirement for development opportunities that enable staff to sustain, manage and advance the academic development of higher education, and the improvement of learning and research environments.

Definitions

Collier identifies four arguments for convergence. The most long-lasting of these is the 'technocratic imperative' argument. This has emerged as the most dynamic of all the arguments and its rationale still applies in 2003. The second, an executive thrust, takes as its raison d'être the need for 'simple lines of authority' for realizing strategic objectives. A third model is that of an information management focus, harmonizing the information generated by an academic community as well as that which it stores by way of recorded knowledge. Finally, Collier suggests the resource management argument that promotes efficient use of areas with similar characteristics.

Collier also illustrates the major consequences that followed early convergence initiatives: the need to identify customer service, management and professional cultures. These issues still dominate debate on convergence but the parameters are being set within different models. The inclusion of an educational technology development and/or an academic staff development unit challenges any traditional notion of convergence. These exist to ensure that academic staff have the opportunity to develop a positive response to the virtual learning environment (VLE). Their staff deny that they are providing a 'service', and finding a common culture can be difficult. This version of convergence produces learning environments that provide a spectrum of services moving from student support, through exploitation and presentation of information and information and communications technologies (ICT), to academic development. IT support and guidance is a normal prerequisite for these learning centres where the general use of computers is actively encouraged. Advice on offer ranges from programme guidance to practical issues of disk management and printing.

Over 15 years of experience now informs the director or manager facing convergence issues. Early adopters included Liverpool John Moores and the Roehampton Institute (London). Some library departments in HEIs have been converged, un-converged, and subsequently realigned with other services (Luton, De Montfort and Northumbria). Others have come late to convergence (for example, Huddersfield in 2001) and, most recently, variations of convergence have emerged in response to developments in teaching and learning, for example in virtual learning environments (Sheffield Hallam, Derby and Lincoln).

One example of a service that has undertaken de-convergence is Luton University. The organization had converged Library, Media and Computing services over a period from early 1990 to January 1993. This brought about an investment in services and a 'consistently high achievement against external audit and assessment' (Stone, 1998). Another benefit was the development of an innovative approach and acceptance of changes in the working environment. However, within five years, other external influences began to be felt, particularly changed government targets, arrangements for financial support of students, and policy initiatives. The services and facilities that made up the newly converged department were disaggregated and locations that were more appropriate to the new university configuration were adopted for printing, education services, and for network and microcomputer support.

Current drivers

In 1997, Phil Sykes and Sarah Gerrard stated, 'Convergence is an optional staging post on an obligatory journey.' Constructive respondents to a study by Lyndon Pugh (1997) commented that the innovation that occurs when different perspectives and knowledge bases are joined is what makes convergence a solution to the unknown and unplanned issues of the future. Those departments that have brought about convergence in the last ten years are well placed in terms of operational effectiveness to deal with the major change experienced in the current pedagogic environment. In the first decade of the 21st century they are likely to refer to a new set of criteria or priorities for meeting university and college strategies. These are the elements of the organization's teaching, learning and assessment strategy. Many academic libraries or learning centres have taken strategic, policy-based decisions about using and exploiting educational and media technology. A teaching, learning and assessment strategy will frequently refer to the learning environment and reflect the importance of their role. These strategies are a pragmatic and unifying solution to the overall issue, whatever organizational forms the convergence takes. However, success would be limited were staff development not factored into the planning stages of organizational or operational change to guarantee staff competence and effective service delivery.

The emergence of HEFCE funds for teaching quality enhancement (TQE) is a significant initiative. It provides a focus on a previously neglected but critical area of academic activity. HEIs bid for and then allocate money to meet broad and specific development needs. This initiative has become a 'movement' in higher education and led to a revival of the alternative learning and teaching (ALT) agenda. The enabling function of ICT has become the catalyst for a paradigm shift in academic practice. New commercial products have emerged to meet the demand for managed learning environments (MLEs) or virtual learning environments (VLEs). Scholarly publication and communication as well as teaching and learning have been transformed by work within an invisible 'net-space'.

The renaissance has affected library and IT systems and support areas in a most significant way. The emergence of a new type of library, as a 'learning centre', is the most tangible outcome. It embraces a new philosophy about the management of and access to resources, the very nature of which have changed. Success has been achieved by attention to resource integration, service culture and management and staff development issues. It was highly appropriate that, following on from the provision of TQE funds, a further innovation was the separate fund for rewarding and developing staff, another HEFCE initiative with money attached. Together, these two are a powerful force for linking staff development to specific developments in the nature of teaching and learning.

Libraries are perhaps more aware and better equipped than most academic departments to deal with the resulting changes in academic delivery via VLEs or MLEs. The experience of changes brought about by convergence has had a positive and progressive effect on the adoption of these 'new' initiatives. Most services have exploited the benefits of having IT or computing elements within or closely aligned with the department. Most library staff have expertise in using IT-based circulation, acquisitions, cataloguing and classification processes, and competence in supporting those using these systems.

Bringing computing staff into the remit of user focused library service departments may have accelerated the growth of IT skills in library staff, but the history of computers in academic libraries suggests that the development of such skills had firm foundations. With HEIs investing in VLEs and MLEs, it has become imperative to find ways of optimizing the benefit of ICT applications to a range of academic services. Computing departments were critical to the success of such initiatives but the balance between technology-driven and technology-based departments has constantly to be revisited in most HEIs during the development period. Another influence on the integration of generic service departments is the promotion of information strategies. Advice to HEIs, issued by the Joint Information Systems Committee (JISC) (1995), advocated collaboration between such services for rational and efficient operations based on informed decision-making.

Convergence of academic support and service departments does not always bring the management of the technical infrastructure into the remit of the academic library or learning centre. According to Edward Oyston (2003), such organizational convergence may bring considerable benefit to overarching information strategies. 'New' convergence is slightly different in that it sets out to maximize the focus on the learner and take forward a strategic learning and teaching agenda. By creating a virtual learning environment, services are integrated into courseware and are accessed via a desktop. Thus, any division between content and operating system is invisible. This is a strong driver for organizational convergence, and brings with it the need for seamless access to system support. Responsibility for computing services has recently migrated to library services at Huddersfield University. The Director of Library Services, Phil Sykes, was previously at Liverpool John Moores and had undertaken a different form of convergence. The strongest driver in this situation is the need for managerial organization to meet the needs of academic development. Having a single department allows strong leadership that can create a service culture and inform the management of staff development to meet user expectations.

Media services have had a slightly different trajectory, frequently arising from a need to maintain collections with appropriate equipment for using them. In some cases, where these materials originated in a production unit, close working relationships were required between producers and keepers if access to the collections was to meet user requirements. Film studies collections and film archives became popular enhancements to library services in the 1980s and along with this came the need to create appropriate learning environments in lecture and classrooms. Many media services units merged with the library services. Examples exist at the Roehampton Institute and Sheffield Hallam University, and different configurations at the universities of East Anglia, Kingston and Stirling. Convergence of media services has been more long lasting and has accommodated a change from media to multi-media in many instances. Some HEIs integrated media production (Sheffield Hallam University), others support users of media technology (University of Lincoln, Roehampton Institute). The new element is that of using media-based courseware production to create learning materials for VLEs. Most HEIs have concluded that this is a relevant service to have alongside other learning facilities and services. It is also a strong argument for the inclusion of educational development units into a learning centre department. Thus, libraries and media services have been retained where computing services may have departed from a unified operation base.

Skills and qualities for convergence and integrated services

Skills analysis

The overall process of convergence needs a variety of skills to meet the subsequent outcomes. In the Joint Funding Councils' Libraries Review Group report, the failure of libraries to provide staff with appropriate training and development was seen as the most important constraint on the implementation of any changes in service development and one that would 'seriously undermine its effectiveness' (1993). Fortunately, it is universally recognized that no initiative starts from a zero skills base. Most directional changes involve a skills audit to enable an assessment of training needs. Although over ten years old, the training guide written by Michael Williamson (1993) provides a sound starting point for the determination of skills training and development needs to meet new challenges. Expertise will be available within any organization and planning should be undertaken with a range of local consultants. These may include the human resources or staff development department, the computing department and the academic development department.

Management skills for new service delivery

Decisions about the nature of the service configuration appropriate for the organization will be taken at senior management level. Once these are agreed, steps need to be taken to ensure that staff in senior positions, responsible for bringing about the required changes, have the right skills to make the initiative work. Converged departments encompass a wide range of services, the nature of the work and the staff are very varied, and consistency of working arrangements are the exception, not the rule. It follows, therefore, that considerable skill is needed to manage them effectively.

It is important to have good communication skills to raise awareness about the new arrangement. Good interpersonal skills, especially in negotiation, are needed to be sufficiently persuasive and, at the same time, reassuring, about the effect change will have on individuals and their working practices.

Much is made of team working in LIS departments. The creation of teams has to be accompanied by team-building exercises and work involving the culture and values to be adopted by teams to achieve organizational objectives. Management development programmes are critical to the success of convergence. The IMPEL project provided good advice in this area (Edwards, Day and Walton, 1998). It identified the factors that are instrumental to best practice in convergence as being:

- communication, horizontal and vertical
- joint staff development and training for shared understanding
- training and management support for staff involved in change

- key post holders acting as change agents
- leadership and clear direction.

Developing and training mangers to be more effective in their responsibilities for staff can improve all of these areas. Senior managers
need to be role models so that all team leaders can benefit from
advice and guidance during a period of change. Working out a statement of common values will help to underpin any development
programme. This solution was put forward by Jan Novak, Associate
Director of Library Services at the Queensland University of
Technology, in a paper to the Vital Link conference in Adelaide
(1999). Novak contends that the changes in the workplace brought
about by a variety of social and economic factors require us to reas-
sure staff by exploring and reaffirming core values of the service.

Skills for the VLE: IT and information skills

A current preoccupation for academic librarians is the integration into
their work of new (technology-based) modes of teaching and learning, and thus confidence in the use of ICT has become an accepted
element of most person specifications. Successful implementation of
new forms of learner support and academic service delivery, needed
by a teaching and learning strategy, will depend on the available skills
of those involved. Work undertaken for the Chartered Institute of
Library and Information Professionals (CILIP) by the author identified the following critical areas of skills, knowledge or expertise
needed in the IT, academic and service areas:

- information technology
- design and creativity
- applications development and use
- systems development and use
- user support (problem solving)
- project management (including people management skills)
  (Fisher, 2002).

The research confirmed the existence of these skills in some areas but not in sufficient quantity to give the required reliability for the future. In the past, it would have been sufficient to focus on developing a combination of IT and information skills for user support at an enquiry desk. More recently, 'library' staff have taken on the element of user support for those migrating to a virtual learning environment. Now the same staff are developing the skills to undertake their traditional roles of information provision via web pages and user education within the VLE. An example of this is the InfoQuest information skills package at Sheffield Hallam University. This generic skills package allows for subject-specific customization and embedding into a 'Blackboard' (Sheffield Hallam University's preferred VLE) programme. Development has been by an academic information specialist and a multimedia courseware developer. The range of skills possessed by these two main players illustrates the skill needs within the learning centre and offers a template for skills acquisition to meet academic development needs.

Susan Fowell and Philippa Levy identified this new professional practice in 1995 (Fowell and Levy, 1995). This followed an examination of 'the virtual library' within the Follett Report (Joint Funding Councils' Libraries Review Group, 1993). As that report predicted, the completely virtual library is rare. However, a growing proportion of library budgets is spent on electronic materials, and for many the medium of the information resource is irrelevant for budgeting purposes. Similarly, for staff in services using a high proportion of IT-based information, skills are needed to exploit and present information as well as retrieve it, whether in electronic or print format. Chapter 2 dealt more specifically with staff development for this important area. This chapter continues by outlining overall generic skills development needs, and ways of meeting them.

Aspects of convergence: the organization of user support systems

Form and function

Staff with the best possible leadership and organizational skills, who are people oriented, are needed to determine the services and systems to be offered within a library and information service. These skills will be at the heart of the service delivered to the users, and critical to the overall success of the department. The comments made by Sheila Corrall and Pat Noon in previous chapters about the skills needed by current and future senior managers are extremely relevant to this issue.

Re-visioning

Each area of library and information operations should have a vision that reflects the values of the parent organization and is translated into a meaningful statement for the service providers. Developed in advance of implementing change, it should be reviewed at regular intervals thereafter. Following six years of learning centre operations at Sheffield Hallam University, changes in the corporate plan of the University have created a need to review services. This is a necessary step to ensure that the staff in the department remain sure of their value to the organization and that the University community continues to trust the department to fulfil an appropriate role and provide effective services and facilities.

Service and customer orientation

Library staff are always seen to have an outward-looking view of the service they offer. Computing staff are perceived to have a view that focuses on getting the technology right for the user. With the emergence of departments that combine the two, at whatever level, there needs to be a common goal for those in the front line of information provision. This can take the form of guidance from staff at enquiry or information desks, or tuition within traditional or virtual class-rooms. It applies to self-managed computer programmes, as well as those mediated by staff. The service standard should be applied consistently. However, much depends on it being articulated in ways that people understand. It is not simply about being polite and adhering to acceptable rules of social engagement. It is more about meeting user expectations within a resource-limited structure. Many staff in academic library services recall previous times when the most experienced staff undertook enquiry desk duties on a common rota. For many contemporary services the expense of such a system outweighs the benefits. Desks are now staffed by personnel trained to deal with a range of enquiries, not by personal knowledge but by a more detailed methodology that includes referring on queries of a specialist nature. This development is a pragmatic answer to the resource issue. It is also an illustration of the changing nature of enquiries within converged services, which are as much about technical issues as information resources.

Training and developing staff for convergence: methods and models

Personal use and understanding

As previously stated, most library and computing staff have considerable experience in the personal use of IT applications (Word, Excel, and so on) and electronic information and bibliographic resources. The application of these skills to situations where staff help users requires a different type of training. Staff need to complement diagnostic skills with instructional skills. Knowledge has to be matched with experience and thus training needs to be affirmed with opportunity to practice. Judgements need to be made about the balance between recognizing existing skills and identifying new ones needed for new roles. In some instances, the 'immersion' method of training will be helpful. It creates a situation where all staff participate in a large-scale programme to ensure that everyone has reached a defined level of skill acquisition. This method also creates stronger ties between members of teams and identifies staff that can mentor those less confident in the use of the new skills.

Applying skills

This second stage of basic IT skills development is critical to the embedding of elementary learning, as outlined above. It should be planned and, if possible, supervised. Sheffield Hallam University and Leeds Metropolitan University employed a supervisor with responsibility for overseeing the skill development of staff. At Sheffield Hallam Learning Centre the secondment of a senior advisor from Computing and Information Services had an additional benefit of giving her experience needed for a teaching certificate. Leeds Metropolitan Learning Support Services created an IT skills developer post to manage departmental skills acquisition. Both departments have subsequently introduced the European Computer Driving Licence course to enable staff to obtain requisite skills. Application of skills is now integrated into personal development plans through appraisal or following up development issues identified during recruitment. The University of Lincoln developed a more structured approach by introducing a competence framework to underpin development in the three areas: behaviour, skills and knowledge (Allan and Reveley, 1999).

Action learning

Action learning is a powerful tool in the staff developer's kit for embedding advanced learning. If users bring 'new' problems to the attention of staff, who then provide answers, it is helpful to all if these answers are shared with others. Technology allows us to use communication methods to record answers or solutions to common problems or frequently asked questions. Many library staff enjoy the notion of recording issues and their solutions for future use. Thus harnessing software programmes for this purpose is popular and effective.

Learning logs are common in student work and portfolios, and personal profiles abound in staff development. Bringing them together to record activities in problem solving is a sensible and useful approach, which will ensure more widespread access to the solutions to common queries.

Qualifications and training programmes

Sheffield Hallam University and Liverpool John Moores University took a similar approach to staff training for a converged service. Analysis of what existed and what was needed was followed by consultation and discussion with staff. Large-scale training programmes were introduced, having been planned and resourced within the implementation plan for convergence. The result was a change in the breadth of the skill base for library and computer staff. There were concerns about the place of professional qualifications, as the standards of professional library qualifications are high and there was no real equivalent in computing. Some staff feared de-skilling and downgrading of posts. In practice posts have been re-evaluated and re-focused on end-users and on the contribution that the change has made to the overall development of learner support. The staff are now multi-skilled and in high demand in most library and information services where integration of IT and information has occurred or is about to happen. This strategy has been applied successfully in many other HEIs and is the overall choice of staff, who have been able to retain their specialist skills when it is adopted.

Planning staff development for convergence

Jo Norry (2003) identifies the development of the following roles and responsibilities for staff in academic libraries, which allow them to meet the needs of student users, concomitant with the changes in teaching and learning strategies and the new focus on the learner as the reference point for service design and delivery:

- Hybridization: multiskilling; integrating IT and library support in one post.
- Providing learner support.
- Integration and partnership with academic staff: integrating IT and information skills capabilities into the curriculum and into learning and teaching techniques.
- Development of library staff as proactive agents of change and innovation in learning and teaching techniques.

These are four main themes for staff development and training in contemporary academic library and information services.

Training needs analysis

It is clear that planning staff development to meet job requirements and personal capabilities is practical and necessary. Williamson (1993) outlines how to approach this. The principles of needs analysis do not change although there is a growing sophistication in the methods used to develop staff. Departmental budgets should be planned to reflect the overall priority needs of service development. Evidence of planned approaches is covered regularly in the *PTEG Journal* (the journal of the Personnel, Training and Education Group of CILIP). One example, used at the University of Lincolnshire and Humberside (now University of Lincoln), is provided by Barbara Allan and Selina Reveley (1999). The need to develop training skills in staff assisting users with information and technological queries is one of the major challenges for successful convergence.

Organization and management of training and development

If training and development are planned, their organization will be simplified. Staff know what to expect, managers know when staff will be undertaking training and resources can be allocated in advance. Evaluation can be set up during and at appropriate times after the activities have been completed. Standards and competences for the information professional in a converged service need to be stated and a popular way of communicating this is in a staff development policy. However, this can be a piece of regulatory paper if not used in conjunction with other tools, staff review and regular training sessions that inform managerial decisions about service or facility development.

Implementing and doing

Responsibility for staff development lies with the line manager and the employee. Although this is generally accepted, if no development takes place it is the manager who takes responsibility for unmet expectations. Table 4.1 illustrates the responsibilities and roles for those involved in the development of library and information practitioners. This table was used to illustrate work for the CILIP into skills and competences for the information professional (Fisher, 2002).

Table 4.1 Roles and responsibilities for the development of library and information practitioners

Individual	Motivation	Credits	Experience
		Qualifications	Skills
			Competences
Educator	Curriculum	Standards	Awards
		Quality	
		Relevance	
Organization	Development and training	Experience	Opportunity
Professional body	Educational and professional qualifications	Accreditation of courses	Linkages
	CPD	Certification of experience	Advocacy

It is clear that there are additional responsibilities for the professional body, and roles for the educators. The provision of CPD courses is a major educational and economic strategy for many learning organizations, and librarians must consider how these needs can be met locally, regionally and nationally. Librarianship is not the only profession that is optimizing technological capability within content-based developments. Museums and archive services are working similarly, and the emergence of the new regional Museums, Libraries and Archives Councils will provide an opportunity to harmonize training initiatives to the benefit of all within these domains. Co-operation in planning and organization of training for convergence could lead to the emergence of a new breed of CPD course. These new courses could be offered as part of an organization's strategic plan, run by a local college or university, accredited by one of the national departments of information and library studies and integrated with service-based practice.

Review through appraisal

Many library departments contain staff who have a mixture of specialist and generalist skills, which develop according to personal and departmental need and in line with strategic imperative. The tool that ensures that these skills will meet user expectations is appraisal or staff review, used in accordance with strategic staff deployment reviews. In order for this to work appropriately, development for line managers and supervisors must be readily available, either within the department or from the central staff development unit of the HEI.

The future

As noted in the introductory section of this chapter, convergence has taken on a new look in the past eight years. The imperative of creating managerial efficiency by converging services has been replaced by the exploitation of technological development in teaching and learning in order to create excellent learning environments for students. There are many influences in this shift. One must be the participation in higher education of many more students with different learning backgrounds. To change the balance between those with compliant learning modes and those with more active responses to learning has required extensive review of methods of teaching and learning.

For many years, it has been apparent that the creators of advertisements have used much more sophisticated media techniques than are employed in educational materials production. This could be attributed to a need to differentiate between leisure products and more academic, intellectual programmes. In viewing media games, younger students are used to a level of interaction that makes learning scenarios look very boring. To match the interaction experienced in games means capitalizing on the techniques available and transferring them to learning situations. This is what is happening in teaching and learning, and library staff need to adopt similar approaches to the essential elements of resource provision and user education. Understanding the psychology of a message is a marketing skill and this indicates another essential area of staff development and training for contemporary services. It also needs staff with skills in creative media techniques, who are in a position to advise academic staff on the integration of ideas with academic content.

Perhaps there is a real convergence occurring in our library and information services in which the agenda for the acquisition of key skills by students is mirroring our own professional need for training and development. The Qualifications and Curriculum Authority (QCA, 2001) identifies the six key skills as:

- Communication
- Information technology
- Application of number
- Working with others
- Improving own learning and performance
- Problem solving.

Conclusion

This chapter has illustrated the development of convergence, from the original need for multi-skilled individuals or teams engaged in service delivery to a broader concept. Those university and college departments where provision of a spectrum of academic support and development leads to the creation of new real and virtual learning environments embody this concept. In all of these scenarios, the essential feature of success is planned and managed staff development appropriate to the identified needs of the individuals who deliver the support to staff and students alike.

References

Allan, B. and Reveley, S. (1999) Developing Training Skills in Learning Support Staff, *PTEG Journal for Library and Information Workers*, **17** (2), (August), 7–9.

Collier, M. (1996) The context of convergence. In Oldroyd, M. (ed.), *Staff Development in Academic Libraries*, London, Library Association Publishing, 68–74.

Edwards, C., Day, J. M. and Walton, G. (eds) (1998) *Monitoring Organisational and Cultural Change: the impact on people of electronic libraries*, The IMPEL2 Project, Newcastle, Joint Information Systems Committee.

Fisher, B. (2002) Report for the Chartered Institute of Library and Information Professionals, unpublished.

Fowell, S. and Levy, P. (1995) Developing a New Professional Practice: a model for networked learner support in higher education, *Journal of Documentation*, **51** (3), 271–80.

Handy, C. (1998) *Beyond Certainty: the changing worlds of organizations*, Harvard, Harvard Business School Press.

John Fielden Consultancy (1993) Supporting Expansion: a report on human resource management in academic libraries for the Joint Funding Councils' Libraries Review Group, Bristol, Higher Education Funding Council for England.

Joint Funding Councils' Libraries Review Group (1993) *Report* (Follett Report), Bristol, Higher Education Funding Council for England.

Joint Information Systems Committee (1995) *Guidelines for Developing an Information Strategy*, Bristol, JISC.

Norry, J. (2003) The Changing Staff Experience. In Oyston, E. (ed.) *Centred on Learning*, Aldershot, Ashgate.

Novak, J. (1999) Affirming Values in a Changing Workplace. In Luzeckyj, A. (ed.) *Vital Link: library staffing in the 21st century. Proceedings of the first Vital Link conference*, University of South Australia and The Australian Library and Information Association, Adelaide, Australia.

Oyston, E. (2003) *Centred on Learning*, Aldershot, Ashgate.

Pugh, L. (1997) *The Convergence of Academic Support Services*, British Library Research and Innovation Centre (BLRIC) Report no. 54, London, British Library.

Qualifications and Curriculum Authority (2001), www.qca.org.uk/.

Stone, T. (1998) (De) Converged Services at Luton, *SCONUL Newsletter*, **14**, 40–1.

Sykes, P. and Gerrard, S. (1997) Operational Convergence at Roehampton Institute London and Liverpool John Moores University, *The New Review of Academic Librarianship*, **3**, 67–89.

Williamson, M. (1993) *Training Needs Analysis*, Library Training Guide, London, Library Association Publishing.

Further reading

British Journal of Academic Librarianship (1988) **3** (3). Articles by Colin Harris, Patrick Kelly and Bernard Naylor.

Fielden, J. (1996) Beyond Fielden: the changing role of information services staff, *Relay*, **43** (Spring), 3–5.

Jordan, P. (1998) *The Academic Library and its User*, Aldershot, Gower.

Philips, S. (1995) *Evaluation*, Library Training Guides, London, Library Association Publishing.

Pinfield, S. (1998) Managing the Hybrid library, *SCONUL Newsletter*, **14**, 41–4.

Pugh, L. (1997) Some Theoretical Bases of Convergence, *New Review of Academic Librarianship*, **3**, 49–66.

Relay (1995) (42) Library and Computing Services. Converge, merge or diverge? Special issue on convergence. Articles by Alistair Duff, Ian Lovecy, Alasdair Paterson, Ivan Sidgreaves, John Slater and Ted Smith.

SCONUL Newsletter (1998) **14** (Autumn).

5

Developing the academic librarian as learning facilitator

Chris Powis

Introduction

Academic libraries have always held a key role in the higher education learning experience but until relatively recently librarians have considered their own role in the process in somewhat limited terms. However, the forces and influences that now shape higher education have led academics and librarians into a more active participation in the learning process, and librarians may now be found working alongside their academic colleagues in facilitating learning inside and outside the library, in physical and virtual spaces. The shift from a support role to an active engagement in the learning process means that academic librarians now need a wider understanding of adult learning and more highly developed teaching skills to fulfil their role. This chapter focuses on the evolving role of the librarian as learning facilitator and teacher of information skills and its implications for staff development needs and routes.

Changing roles

In the UK major changes in the teaching and learning role of the academic librarian first came about with the advent of easily accessible and relatively cheap research databases in the late 1980s. Although there had been exceptions, for example tutor librarians in some polytechnics, the principal contact between librarian and student before this was during induction and then, subsequently, over an enquiry desk. It was still the academic who usually guided and influenced students in finding information for specialist subjects. As the routes to information became more plentiful, and superficially more complicated, academics found it less easy to maintain this role and librarians found themselves, reluctantly in some cases, taking a more active part in student instruction. Fielden, recognizing this change, noted that technological advances meant a role for library staff in passing on their ability to access information, and that subject librarians would have to understand teaching and learning (HEFCE, 1993). As early adopters of new technology, librarians were well placed to understand and use the internet as a tool for the exploitation of information and the delivery of learning activities as it grew during the 1990s. Institutional, governmental and market forces made e-learning a major driver in course development over this period and librarians needed to develop and maintain their expertise in using this medium. The same period saw library staff working much more closely with their IT, media or learning technology counterparts, in some cases in converged services. Librarians became used to working with colleagues from academic and other support departments to create effective learning opportunities for students.

Changing context

Change in the nature of the student body and in patterns of learning also influenced the role of the librarian in the learning process. Modular courses and programmes have fractured the course cohesion that allowed subject librarians to work closely with one cohort of students. Liaison between librarian and academic over information skills training became more difficult to co-ordinate and the potential for students to be taught the same thing several times increased. The Dearing Report (NCIHE, 1997) articulated the trend towards the development of key academic skills training, and although information skills were not identified in the report, there was a clear opportunity to use the climate of greater acceptance of key skills to raise the profile of information skills. Modularity created opportunities for stand-alone, information-related modules in response to the increased acceptance of the key skills and employability agenda, which gathered pace through the 1990s, reinforced by the inclusion of skills within subject benchmarks. Developments in Australia and the USA, enthusiastically embraced by SCONUL and others in the UK (Town, 2000), widened the emphasis to include information literacy, adding evaluation, organization, communication and synthesis to the usual array of library information skills. A growth in part-time and distance-learning students, allied to the increasing need for full-time students to work to support their studies, has meant that the learning opportunities offered by librarians have had to be taken out of traditional physical and temporal limits. The encouragement of mature students into higher education has led to the growth of a body of students demanding and needing more help in accessing and understanding information. This trend has been accelerated with the widening participation agenda, introducing students who have much greater need for guidance and support in their learning. The importance of retaining students to the provision of funding has led to a greater student focus with a consequent growth of interest in the holistic student experience, a process in which the library has a key role. The growth in student numbers and the research assessment exercise (RAE) have necessitated changes to the amount of support that academics can give individuals, and made the adoption of teaching and learning strategies based around group or individual study more prevalent than that based on small seminar or tutorial groups. All these factors have meant that librarians are facing large groups of students who increasingly need structured and detailed assistance in learning how to learn, as well as how to access information, and who may demand such help 24/7. Alison Hudson (2003) has noted that higher education 'requires effective learning and teaching strategies if diverse groups of students are not to be disempowered, alienated or marginalised'. This is as true on the micro level of information skills and literacy as it is of higher education as a whole.

The learning facilitator

The concept of a learning facilitator has been developing in response to the changing nature of the HE environment and its effect on the academic librarian's role. Discussed in Dearing and other reports, a major influence on the idea was the JISC-funded eLib programme with projects like TapIN, NetLinks and Netskills (eLib, n.d.) identifying a mixture of IT and teaching and learning skills needed to adapt to their new environment. It was also clear that librarians would need to work closely with academics and other departments, in teaching teams, to deliver the support needed. This did not necessarily mean a complete change of role to become teachers, as the traditional librarian's set of organizational, mediating and navigational skills was also needed to facilitate learning in an increasingly complex information landscape (Elkin, 1999).

The librarian's role as a learning facilitator in this changing environment has many facets. The teaching and learning support team offering inductions, workshops, seminars and other types of learning event is well established. Usually operating outside a formal course or module structure but possibly linked to a particular information need or assignment, and dependent on good liaison between librarians and academics, this has been the staple of subject team teaching for at least 20 years. Usually running alongside this is one-to-one work with students, sometimes via formal tutorials or an enquiry desk and often also through an informal drop-in arrangement. More and more librarians are now also becoming involved in formal teaching, either as part of a skills element within an 'academic' course or as teachers on separate information-related modules. This involves librarians becoming more involved in 'academic' issues like assessment with all the attendant quality requirements.

It should not be forgotten that librarians have a staff development role within institutions. This can be internal to the department as the changing information environment demands almost constant updating, but also external in relation to other university staff or within the LIS profession. Indeed, librarians operating in partnership with staff development or other support units can now be seen delivering parts of courses on teaching and learning to new academic staff. For all these methods to work effectively, close liaison between librarian and academic is needed, and strategic links need to be made between the objectives of the learning event and the needs of the whole institution.

The growth in e-delivery of information and resources has created a situation where, as the JISC (2003) has noted, 'learning technology is now the context in which they were applying their professional skills'. As forms of e-learning begin to become normal in all modes of higher education delivery, including full-time campus based courses, an understanding of the different skills and knowledge required to develop online learning is becoming essential. Many librarians are skilled in developing online learning environments, as evidenced by the number of information portals there are, and this often gives them insights into the use of VLEs and other online environments that are useful in informing institutional debates on online learning. Such skills should be encouraged and used if libraries are not to be sidelined, but there is a need to make sure that e-learning is pedagogically and not technologically driven. The impetus towards online learning therefore highlights the need for more multi-disciplinary teams to work in higher education, with librarians taking a role alongside IT specialists, learning technologists and academics. The skills needed for this type of working should also be prioritized alongside a recognition of the implications for teaching and learning of a more academically, socially and culturally diverse student body.

Formal development routes

The role of the academic librarian in facilitating learning has clearly changed and is continuing to develop. However, the curriculum offered by departments of Library and Information Studies does not seem to reflect this. The subjects offered by all CILIP-accredited institutions reflect a change in the IT skills base required by those entering the profession, but little if anything in the way of teaching skills is delivered. Unless they have previously completed a teaching qualification, those newly entering academic libraries have little understanding of the pedagogical issues or practical skills needed to facilitate learning effectively. In itself this is no different from most new academics starting their careers, as identified by Dearing and others, but it is surely a missed opportunity. The lifelong learning agenda, and the desire to empower all sections of the community and workforce to access information effectively, means that it is not just those entering academic libraries who will need to facilitate learning. All newly qualified information workers need to be equipped to function in this role.

Consequently, teaching skills in academic libraries have traditionally been learned on the job. New librarians are usually pitched into a teaching session with little formal preparation save the opportunity to observe someone else doing something similar. They will often be delivering someone else's material and rarely have the skills necessary to produce something new themselves. If they are fortunate they will be working in a sympathetic team or with a mentor who will encourage reflection and debate about teaching and learning, and they will be able to develop alongside their peers. The needs of the department and the pressure of student numbers often militate against anything other than this approach and, to some extent, it mirrors the experience of the new academic. Some people clearly thrive in this environment and if carefully supported there need be no noticeable drop in the effectiveness of the learning experience for students. However, there remains the need for a more formal framework for developing that knowledge and understanding if it is to be embedded in practice.

Dearing identified the need for more formal training for new academics, and most universities now include attendance on an accredited teaching course as a contractual obligation for new teaching staff. These are usually at Postgraduate Certificate or Diploma level but may be at Masters, are taught in-house, and the most usual accreditation comes from the Institute for Learning and Teaching in Higher Education (ILTHE) or the Staff and Educational Development Association (SEDA). Membership of bodies like the ILTHE is open to librarians and should be considered as it provides access to a national network of those interested in a greater professionalism in teaching and learning in higher education. Conferences run by ILTHE, SEDA and others provide excellent content and the chance to develop alongside colleagues from outside the information world. There are other specialist teaching qualifications, many offered online, which could either be taken as a top-up or as an alternative. Most universities offer a Certificate in Education (Cert. Ed.) course while other more specialized courses are offered by institutions like the Institute of Education (University of London) or the Open University. Librarians are often to be found taking these courses, and even on the course teams, and this integration with academic staff can provide considerable benefits for both parties. However, there have been problems in librarians gaining access to such courses in some institutions on the grounds that they 'do not teach'. This has, in extreme cases, led to librarians having an input to courses that they cannot join.

A problem with such courses is that they do not usually recognize the differences in the teaching done by librarians and other academic support staff. Although many librarians do formally assess student work, many do not and have to rely on more informal, formative methods of assessment. Many librarians also have limited access to the students they teach, typically seeing them for a few hours at most, and this can lead to difficulties with auditing knowledge, group dynamics and identifying learning styles and needs. Few courses recognize these differences and, although many are portfolio based and experience driven, the taught elements can be less forgiving of different teaching patterns.

Formal training in teaching skills within a library context is rare but not completely unknown. The JISC-funded Edulib Project ran from

1996 until 1999 and delivered training to around 250 librarians nation-wide, with the intention that it would cascade down through their institutions. Although surveys for Edulib (Core, 1999) and the Big Blue project (Big Blue, n.d.) identified a demand for such training, provision has been patchy since the end of Edulib in 1999. Organizations such as CILIP, Aslib and the Oxford Centre for Staff Development have also run workshops, as have specialist subject groups like the HeLIN network of health libraries (Palmer, 1996). Professional groups, conferences and networking are important for spreading good practice and sparking ideas, for example, the workshops and meetings of organizations such as CILIP's University, College and Research Group (UC&R). The great advantage of such courses is that the workshops recognize the different context that librarians work in, and offer a 'safer' environment for staff to discuss issues that affect them in their teaching. When used as an additional strand to more formal academic courses these can work well, but they can reinforce feelings of isolation from mainstream teaching and learning activity. Librarians should not feel that their professional identity is under threat if they seek development opportunities outside the comfort zone of library-oriented events. Although some librarians may feel somewhat intimidated in an academic-dominated environment, this is precisely where they should be operating if they are to be taken seriously as teachers and learning facilitators.

The success of Edulib and other similar courses is partly based on the application of practice to training, and this raises the issue of the timing of such courses. Should librarians wait until they have experience of teaching before embarking on formal, or semi-formal, training or should it come first so that they have a grounding in theory before finding themselves in front of a class? In the case of new academics most will be teaching, perhaps with a mentor as support, while undertaking a teaching qualification and it would seem appropriate for this model to apply to subject librarians. However, academics would not normally have the opportunity of a qualification in 'being an academic', while virtually all subject librarians will have been through an accredited course in librarianship or information work.

Some grounding in theory and practice within such courses would enable new staff to approach their duties and their academic colleagues with confidence.

Other development routes

Librarians have access to a range of other staff development opportunities, which although not necessarily badged as being about teaching and learning are important in developing them as learning facilitators. Where possible staff should take the opportunity to teach in teams, with colleagues and with academics, and to add peer observation to their existing feedback mechanisms. Team teaching and peer observation are valuable tools in developing an individual's teaching both as observed and observer. Contributing to the wider teaching and learning activity of the institution can be immensely useful in developing the role of learning facilitator by working alongside academic colleagues. Librarians should seize the chance to take part in institutional teaching and learning initiatives, committees and events. They should make themselves aware of and attend conferences, professional events and workshops in teaching and learning. Judith Peacock (2000) notes the importance of participation in high level teaching and learning activities and the role of mentoring by senior staff in encouraging strategic skills in the area. Librarians should seek opportunities to take part in course development and in teaching quality enhancement activities, not just to represent the library, but also to learn from and take part in debates about teaching and learning.

Development in learning and teaching should not be confined to subject librarians or similar staff. All staff should feel that they have a role in facilitating learning. Although the delivery of courses, workshops and other learning events tends to be dominated by subject teams, others within the library have a part to play as learning facilitators. Students may not recognize the differences between the functions of library staff and will seek help where they can find it. At the very least, all staff should be aware of the role of the library in the learning process and be able to facilitate the student progressing in some way, if only by referral to the appropriate source of help, or in using the catalogue. Awareness-raising events, job shares or shadowing, regular communications about teaching and learning, can help all staff to understand their part in the overall process.

Conclusion

The role of the librarian in facilitating learning is developing relatively quickly, and it is perhaps a good time to take stock of where we have come from and what we need to do to maintain a role in the learning landscape of our institutions. Roles are increasingly blurred as more work is done in multi-disciplinary teams, and we should be reflecting this in the increased integration of our development as teachers and learning facilitators. Opportunities for joint development with academics on formal accredited courses in teaching should be sought, and membership of the ILTHE and similar bodies taken out where appropriate. Librarians do often teach in a different context to academics with shorter contact hours and limited experience of assessment. The message from EduLib and similar providers of courses is that they are keen to have a library context to their training in this area. This is no different from academics working with learning and teaching support network centres or special interest groups in their subjects. The changing nature of delivery, and of the student body, means that issues of diversity and e-learning will need to be addressed by all in higher education, and librarians' experience in dealing with these in a library context means that they have much to offer in the current debate. Allied to the need for development is also the need for adequate reward for developing roles, and the profession as a whole needs to address this. Librarians should not be trying to become academics but they should be rewarded appropriately for the part they play in the learning process. Library staff are operating in a different environment now and everyone working in an academic library needs to recognize their role in facilitating learning and to grasp the development opportunities that this offers.

References

Big Blue, www.leeds.ac.uk/bigblue/.

Core, J. (1999) EduLib: the programme closes but lives on, *Relay*, **48**, 14.

eLib: the Electronic Libraries Programme, www.ukoln.ac.uk/services/elib/.

Elkin, J. (1999) The Role of the Librarian in Learning and Teaching in Higher Education, *Relay*, **48**, 7–9.

Higher Education Funding Council for England (1993) *Supporting Expansion: a report on human resource management in academic libraries for the Joint Funding Councils' Libraries Review Group* (Fielden Report), Bristol, HEFCE.

Hudson, A. (2003) New Environments: the environment for learning. In Oyston, E., *Centred on Learning: academic case studies on information centre development*, Aldershot, Ashgate.

The Joint Information Systems Committee (2003) *Learning Technology: key implications for library staff*, www.jisc.ac.uk/uploaded_documents/ Briefing5_Library_services_finalcopy_JW.doc.

National Committee of Inquiry into Higher Education (1997) *Higher Education in the Learning Society* (Dearing Report), London, HMSO.

Palmer, J. (1996) Skills for the Millennium – the Librarian of the 21st Century, *Librarian Career Development*, **4** (1), 13–17.

Peacock, J. (2000) *Teaching Skills for Teaching Librarians: postcards from the edge of the educational paradigm*, http://archive.alia.org.au/sections/uclrs/aarl/32.1/fulltext/ peacock.html.

Town, S. (2000) Wisdom or Welfare: the seven pillars model. In Corrall, S. and Hathaway, H. (eds), *Seven Pillars of Wisdom? Good practice in information skills development*, London, Society of College, National and University Libraries.

6

Development routes for academic library support staff

Jo Webb

Introduction

The crucial and changing role of academic library support staff is recognized throughout this chapter, which reviews the shifting nature of their work and the development opportunities that this necessitates. Training and development methods for these staff in the UK are considered including a range of new certificated courses such as the Information and Library Services National Vocational Qualifications (ILS NVQs). The need for a holistic and strategic approach to support staff training and development is emphasized.

Support staff roles

To a large extent library support staff shape the customer experience of all who visit academic libraries. Support staff work on issue counters, sometimes other service points, and are responsible for shelving operations as well as much of the day-to-day work that underpins the service encounter. They form the largest proportion of library and information staff and are the most diverse group in age profile, educational background, expectations, working patterns, ethnicity and more.

Yet support staff are an invisible majority in written strategy and policy, rarely mentioned in discussions of human resource management in libraries. This is not uncommon: compare the amount written on any level of management development compared with that for administrative staff in business or the public sector. In practice consideration of the training needs of this group of staff is less widely ignored, although relatively little attention is given to their development.

The academic library world is one in which there is usually a separation between qualified staff and others. The divide is harder to maintain in converged services, but progression without some form of graduate-level qualification in a cognate area is unusual. Senior staff often have underlying values of difference, of separateness, of a sense that, 'We can all too easily divide our work ... and assume that junior staff can only be expected to do the simple, routine, repetitive, and often frankly boring work' (Burch, 1980, 5).

Writing seven years after Burch, in a study on the same theme, David Baker (1987) explored the development of paraprofessional qualifications. He reviewed the tension between elitist professional approaches to management and education, compared with more inclusive approaches in the past, and concluded that status distinctions led to task and role distinction. The graduate (and increasingly postgraduate) qualification barrier has reinforced this separation, even when academic libraries employ large numbers of highly qualified support staff. The development of paraprofessional qualifications has only rarely opened up career structures for able support staff. Perhaps at times it is assumed that anyone who is not a qualified librarian is less motivated or interested in the work they do than their qualified colleagues. Yet there is huge commonality of work, and most of the time the duties of qualified librarians overlap with or depend on input from library support staff.

At the same time as professional exclusivity is maintained, managers are adopting more holistic approaches to staff management and training. These approaches reflect the desire for improved organizational performance and more people-centred human resource management practice. At an institutional level there are clear drivers for these changes, notably the increasing importance of student feedback and satisfaction within academic quality enhancement, the need to manage declining resources, and making difficult decisions in times of uncertainty and change. There are institutional efforts to change management culture to improve the use and development of soft skills and value-centred leadership. The recent developments of institutional HR strategies and the numbers of services bearing the Investors in People or Charter Mark accreditations provide clear evidence of this. Investors in People, in particular, requires evidence of strategic alignment between human resources and service objectives at every level of the organization. The Charter Mark, built around service excellence, must by its very nature require all staff to reach specific standards of service.

Much of this work is known only through professional networking. It is rarely reported in the literature or reflected in external staff development events, and little commented on except in the Fielden report (John Fielden Consultancy, 1993).

Other chapters of this book discuss the changing roles of staff working in academic libraries in more detail, but it may be useful to comment briefly on the impact of these changes on the activities and roles of support staff. It is very difficult to generalize about exactly what work is done by support or qualified staff. There are so many differences between organizations and even service points within the same organization. Nevertheless there are some common trends. Boundaries between the work done by qualified and support staff have shifted. Qualified librarians have moved away from direct customer contact, so that support staff do most lending and enquiry work. IT and computing staff are replacing systems specialists, and much of the work in cataloguing and acquisitions sections has been simplified, streamlined and automated, reducing the need for qualified staff input. Even in traditional domains like lending services, the introduction of self-issue is changing the nature of work for all involved. The recent work edited by Oyston (2003) is a useful source of case studies detailing these shifts in role.

Support staff roles have become more complex. Often support staff work in matrix structures, combining work on service desks together with work in a subject or functional team. The duties in each area are now more diverse. This reflects the increased range of activities and functions within modern academic libraries, from converged information and learning support to more targeted and segmented services, all within very different physical environments from those of 20 or even ten years ago. This trend is not likely to stop. The intensity of detail required of many digital library developments means that libraries need skilled but cost-effective staff to do much of the work fundamental for success.

Equally, managers are more aware of the benefits of staff training and development. There are tangible skill improvements, but also increased flexibility, motivation and more positive attitudes to change (Whetherly, 1998). Training and development deliver tangible benefits to the organization, create a richer work environment for library users and all who work there and help to future-proof staff in times of increasing change (Harrison, 2002; Marchington and Wilkinson, 2002).

Types of development opportunities

Let us now turn from the rhetoric to a more specific discussion of the types of development suitable, relevant and appropriate for library support staff. These categories are used for clarity of explanation only, rather than being a fixed typology.

Competence-based development

Competence-based development enables an individual staff member, group or team to work more effectively. Exactly what the training and development will comprise may depend on organizational priorities or service objectives, but they can be summarized in the following ways:

- *Technical, professional and specific skills* This group includes enhancing the use of particular systems or operations, for example functions of the library management system, acquisition routines, use of specialist equipment, health and safety
- *Interpersonal and communication skills* Soft skills are increasingly recognized as being important in the workplace, both at the highest level where Goleman (1998) claims that emotional intelligence is more important that other intelligence, to skills for dealing with particular parts of the working life. Recognized areas for support staff training include, for example, customer care, enquiry handling and team working.
- *Management of oneself and others* This includes a range of topics from supervisory skills to time management and stress management.
- *Wider awareness of the organizational context* This may include understanding the operations of related departments (like the registry) or linked organizations (like suppliers) or briefings about the mission and role of the institution. Visits to other organizations, which can provide opportunities to take stock, identify good practice and reflect on how things are done at your own institution, could also be included.

Career enhancement

Careers may be enhanced through promotion as a member of library support staff (although studies in the 1980s and 1990s identified the absence of more senior support posts as a major cause of dissatisfaction) (Russell, 1985; Thapisa, 1989; Thapisa 1991). Equally career enhancement may take the form of someone qualifying as a librarian, either full-time or part-time, or acquiring qualifications or recognizing skills and abilities that would translate well into other work environments.

Personal development

The final type of development opportunity relates to personal development, through improved motivation or job enrichment. These humanistic values can seem contrary to the business-focused objectives discussed earlier, but it is not merely platitudinous to suggest that more motivated and stimulated staff are better at their work; most research on motivation confirms this theory (Jordan and Lloyd, 2002).

It can be too easy to assume, perhaps especially within the divided world already discussed, that people in support roles, apart from those who are graduate trainees, have limited ambitions. This can particularly seem the case when you encounter staff who are resistant to training or development, adopting a functionalist approach to their work. Yet, in my personal experience (and tested in a small-scale research project in the late 1990s), library support staff share just the same achievement motivation as qualified librarians.

The range of training and development activities described so far can be defined as a matrix, ranging knowledge and skills against individual or organizational learning, as shown in Figure 6.1. Although simplistic, the matrix illustrates the range of opportunities that can be provided.

Knowledge	[e.g. Disability awareness]	[e.g. Organizational mission]
Skills	[e.g. Interpersonal skills]	[e.g. Technical skills]
	Individual	Organization

Figure 6.1   A matrix for staff development opportunities

Training and development methods

If we have identified the outcomes of the development opportunities, we need to turn to development methods. Just as a matrix was used to classify the purposes of development, it is important to be aware that there are many different ways of developing staff. Rather than a mechanistic, 'If you need training on Y you should attend course X', managers should select training and development methods that match individual and organizational needs and objectives. The diversity of the workforce means that managers cannot and should not assume that training and development needs can be fixed by attending courses. Staff development policies and practice should reflect a much broader understanding of how staff development (and adult learning) can be achieved. Creth (1986), Goulding and Kerslake (1997) and Lobban (1997) all provide excellent discussions of how to plan and organize workplace training, and anyone wishing to explore these ideas further should refer to these sources.

Proactive approaches to staffing and staff development through line management can be the most powerful way of developing all library staff. Team and matrix organizational structures are particularly effective at creating opportunities for just this sort of work, as long as we recognize the positive contribution all levels and grades of staff make to organizational success. In our ever-changing environment, many work activities can be seen as an opportunity for individual learning and development and improved effectiveness. Even once-simple tasks like checking reading lists can be development opportunities, involving use of a range of bibliographic and full-text databases and reading list software programs.

Line managers can develop their support staff in several ways. The most simple development route is through task allocation: delegating more complex tasks to these staff (and supporting them in completing the work) or rotating duties or responsibilities. In large academic libraries there is often increased specialization, so re-allocating work duties also enables staff to develop a broader skills base and thus increase their flexibility. Another route can be through involvement in working parties, projects and special groups. Given the trend for qualified staff to withdraw from overseeing technical operations and much customer contact, support staff can offer accurate insights and analysis of what is happening in practice.

Management style can be an influential factor in achieving this. In Sykes's words, 'There is no point…in training up a cadre of self-starting and creative assistants…if the real power structure of the organization is authoritarian and centralist, and middle and senior managers are expected to manage in a dully prescriptive and mechanistic way' (1996, 90). A democratic, inclusive approach to determining the work of the team or the department, or even in objective-setting, can involve and engage all staff in their work, and ensure that front-line concerns and knowledge are integrated into organizational objectives. The self-managed team (Yeatts and Hyten, 1998), although difficult to achieve in practice, can be a very effective way of achieving learning and development for all.

With increased responsibility comes personal development, and the benefits of working as trainers or supervisors should not be under-estimated. Often the people who do the work day-to-day make the best trainers. Rather than a section manager showing a new member of staff how a particular piece of software works, why not let the assistant who uses it every day show the new colleague?

But training is not necessarily development. For development to take place the training must serve individual needs and also organizational objectives. These can be co-ordinated most effectively through formal policies that serve to address staff training and development concerns and reflect organizational objectives and targets as well (Murray and Oldroyd, 2002). The staff development policy should lead to the establishment of a co-ordinated programme of training events, and clarification of how to get access to training and development opportunities, in ways that are sensitive to the needs of the whole workforce.

Many of the policies published in Murray and Oldroyd identify a wide range of approaches to training and development, including work shadowing, job rotation and job exchanges. It is important to include informal as well as formal development methods and to emphasize that everyone should make time available for their learning and development. Many organizations make this practice explicit either through arranging specific training hours or through self-directed learning time. At De Montfort University, for example, everyone is allocated an annual number of training time entitlement hours to spend on learning and development opportunities. Open learning packages and programmes can make it easier to structure this self-directed learning as can using online packages, especially if people find it difficult to attend a formal face-to-face training event. The Open University's assessed MOSAIC online module, or its free version Safari, are good examples of online learning materials relevant to staff wishing to develop their information-searching skills (Open University, n.d.)

The potential learner needs to be very motivated to complete open or self-directed programmes of study. One of the benefits of undertaking a course leading to a formal qualification is that learning and development opportunities are structured and shaped by the curriculum, the tutor or assessor, and the assessment process. Several library and information-based courses combine workplace assessment and practice into externally recognized qualifications.

Information and Library Services National Vocational Qualifications

Information and Library Services National Vocational Qualifications (ILS NVQs) are perhaps the best known externally recognized qualifications for support staff in LIS in the UK. Launched in 1995, ILS NVQs are competence-based qualifications (Winkworth et al., 1999). Candidates compile portfolios of evidence in order to demonstrate that they have reached levels of occupational competence and can demonstrate knowledge in clearly defined activities like circulation, dealing with enquiries or using IT. Each candidate has an assessor and the work is also verified internally and externally. ILS NVQs are learner-centred. Rather than following a prescriptive assessment rubric, candidates can select what evidence they wish to use to complete each unit of the NVQ and they can work at their own pace. This means that NVQs are potentially accessible to a very wide range of library support staff, including solo workers and people on part-time and fractional contracts. The comprehensive range of units is built around a core covering essential elements of library and information work with options in areas like display management, IT and handling enquiries.

When first introduced there were three levels of ILS NVQ. Level 2 is the entry level, designed for library assistants who do not have supervisory responsibility. Level 3 is suitable for staff who have some management or supervisory responsibility or who wish to progress from their level 2 award. Level 4 was equivalent to part of a degree, and it was hoped that it would provide an opportunity for library support staff to become qualified librarians. Sadly, with a change in awarding body and the introduction of revised standards, Level 4 was lost, just as CILIP's professional qualifications framework is opening up access.

The INSIST report (Parker, Hare and Gannon-Leary, 1999) was a comprehensive evaluation of ILS NVQs. The research team found that ILS NVQs offered personal and skills development, and stimulated innovation and improved customer service within the workplace. They concluded:

> The training and development [provided by NVQs] is structured, assessed, evaluated and – most importantly – recognised and celebrated. It is the structure, the evaluation of the development, the consistent feedback and the recognition of achievement that makes NVQs so much more valuable than conventional training programmes.

In summary, if support staff work on the units leading to ILS NVQs successfully they can achieve many of the staff development outcomes defined in the matrix discussed earlier: benefits for the individual and the organization, in increased knowledge and skill levels.

De Montfort University was one of the participants in the Impact of NVQs in Information and Library Services on Library Staff

Induction and Staff Training (INSIST) research project, having been an ILS NVQ assessment centre since 1996. NVQ Levels 2 and 3 have been offered to library staff, with assessment and internal verification provided in-house. Over 20 support staff have achieved a qualification at Level 2 or 3, and ten staff were enrolled on the ILS NVQ programme in 2003. Almost every possible demographic group has been represented in our list of successful candidates: school leavers, part-time evening staff, full-time assistants, term-time only staff and more. Until 2002, there was no direct incentive to undertake the qualification. Since then progression criteria have been revised and possession of NVQs at Level 2 and 3, or an equivalent qualification, became mandatory to progress to Scale 3 or 4 respectively. Despite the absence of a tangible reward, many candidates derived clear benefits from following the ILS NVQ programme, from improved career opportunities, changed roles or improved recognition or awareness of their work context.

Another benefit to the organization, mentioned less frequently in the published literature, is that NVQs offer development opportunities for assessors as well as candidates. If, as at De Montfort University, line managers are used as NVQ assessors, two kinds of development take place at the same time. The ILS NVQ candidates work towards their qualifications, while the assessors (who must also have their own NVQ in assessment) gain experience of mentoring, coaching, assessment and quality enhancement. These assessor skills are of increasing value in the workplace, especially as more human resource management is devolved to line managers, and as library staff become more involved in teaching, learning and assessment themselves.

Other certificated courses

Rather than adopting NVQs, two regional groups developed their own certificated staff development programmes, aimed mainly at support staff. Both programmes are built around formal teaching sessions and summative assessment, rather than the largely competence-based, portfolio-led approach of NVQs. The NoWAL

(North West Academic Libraries) consortium developed a Certificate in Library and Information Practice (CLIP), accredited by the Greater Manchester Open College Network (Mackenzie, 2002; Young, 2003). Consisting of five units, covering library and information skills, IT, internet, managing self and others and customer service skills, this is a modular course combining a mixture of teaching and self-directed study. The units can be taken in any order over a five-year period in order to achieve the final award. Since CLIP started 119 people have registered to take units and between them they have achieved 283 credits. Of these 106 people were working as library support staff and they have achieved 255 credits between them. By July 2003 six people had obtained the full certificate and another 21 were close to completion.

Some of the feedback from CLIP participants provides clear evidence of the developmental benefits accrued: 'I really enjoyed this course. I was very apprehensive beforehand, as I have not studied for over 10 years … I am encouraged to take on further studies and would like to do other CLIP courses.' 'CLIP has given me the confidence to apply for a part-time BA Hons Degree in Information and Library Management.'

The School of Information Management at Leeds Metropolitan University offers a Certificate in Information and Library Studies (CILS). This was developed to meet a need for continuing professional development in the Yorkshire region. Local libraries advise the School on staff development needs in the region and in turn the School has access to a pool of potential students whose employers support their attendance one day a week on the programme (Norry, 2003). The Certificate has four modules: the library in society, assessing user needs, cataloguing and indexing, and IT and the presentation of information. The qualification is perceived as being a route onto the degree programme as well as potentially linking into CILIP membership.

Both courses combine the work-based focus of the NVQ with more traditional taught elements. The long-established City and Guilds Information and Library Studies Award 7370 is another qualification aimed at library and information staff. It has a traditional syllabus based around the principal organizational routines and practices required in running libraries or information units. Syllabus areas include selecting, storing, stocking and maintaining materials, assisting users to locate and retrieve information, personal presentation and communication. Learners normally attend a local college on day release and work on assignments that they can link to their current duties and responsibilities.

More recently Foundation Degrees and Modern Apprenticeships are government initiatives to improve the level of vocational training within the workforce and they combine workplace learning with formal study. They are so far untested within academic libraries, and at the time of writing (2003) no foundation degrees in library and information work have been validated.

Much of the discussion of training and development for library support staff has focused on the 'career library assistant' (Russell, 1985; Webb, 1990) rather than including the person who wishes to qualify as a librarian, as Ollerenshaw (2001) rightly points out. Traditionally this is because graduate trainees went to 'library school', so the aspiring librarians were rarely identified as people who might look for additional staff development beyond their training year, apart from a minority of people who were sponsored to study part-time locally before moving into qualified posts.

Anecdotally, in 2003 it appears that fewer academic library employers are able or prepared to finance support staff on CILIP-accredited courses. Yet part-time students working in academic libraries are much more likely to stay in the same sector. This is especially the case if they have received support for their CPD (Ollerenshaw, 2001, 175). Given increasing concerns over the age profile of the profession and numbers of applicants for posts, it seems like a missed opportunity. It would be unfair to blame LIS employers: fewer employers sponsor courses not directly related to current duties, and there is a greater expectation of self-funding further study.

The final area for formal training and development is in studying for other qualifications. These may be NVQs in subjects like customer service, or the popular European Computer Driving Licence (ECDL) for IT, which are of direct relevance to the job. Alternatively, the qualifications may be developmental, for example support to do a course within the institution, which is not directly related to library and information work, like an HND or Foundation Degree in business.

Conclusion

Library support staff are no longer 'treated with studied indifference' (MacDougall, 1986, 41) and there are excellent accounts of good training practice, and widespread recognition of the value of staff development. Yet many of the accounts and perhaps much of the current practice focuses on training rather than development and takes a rather instrumental approach to both processes. Nearly every academic library will make available some competence-based training and development for support staff, but often this is built upon employer priorities and voluntary participation, rather than linking into personal development needs and organizational strategy.

There is little published evaluation of the impact of training and development activities on the work and motivation of library support staff, nor on the organization as a whole and, apart from success in programmes like Investors in People, little evidence of the development of performance indicators or self-assessment. There are then three challenges ahead. At a practical level, all staff must be encouraged to take responsibility and be given opportunities to learn and develop themselves. In turn, line managers must recognize that they have a critical role in shaping their team's training and development, both through formal courses and work-based activities, and that this human resource development role is a core part of their responsibilities. Finally, employers must establish frameworks and policies that draw together individual learning and organizational development, learning from the best practice in success areas like ILS NVQs.

Notes

My thanks to Gil Young of NoWAL and Jo Norry of Leeds Metropolitan University for the information provided about CLIP and the Leeds Metropolitan Certificate.

References

Baker, D (1987) *Certificates in Library Work: an historical-critical study of non-professional level librarianship qualifications in Britain, with reference to other countries, professions and training schemes*, unpublished PhD thesis, Loughborough, Loughborough University of Technology.

Burch, B. (1980) [Untitled]. In Baker, D. (ed.), *Junior Staff Training: papers read at a meeting of the East Midlands branch of the University College and Research Section of the Library Association held on 26 March 1980 at Leicester University Library*, Leicester, UCRS of the Library Association (East Midlands Branch), 4–8.

Creth, S. (1986) *Effective On-the-job Training*, Chicago, American Library Association.

Goleman, D. (1998) *Working with Emotional Intelligence*, London, Bloomsbury.

Goulding, A. and Kerslake, E. (1997) *Training for Part-time and Temporary Workers*, Library Training Guide, London, Library Association Publishing.

Harrison, R. (2002) *Learning and Development*, 3rd edn, London, Chartered Institute of Personnel and Development.

John Fielden Consultancy (1993) *Supporting Expansion: a report on human resource management in academic libraries for the Joint Funding Councils' Libraries Review Group*, Bristol, Higher Education Funding Council for England.

Jordan, P. and Lloyd, C. (2002) *Staff Management in Library and Information Work*, 4th edn, Aldershot, Ashgate.

Lobban, M. (1997) *Training Library Assistants*, Library Training Guide, London, Library Association Publishing.

MacDougall, A. (1986) Training Provision in Academic Libraries. In Prytherch, R. (ed.), *Staff Training in Libraries: the British experience*, Aldershot, Gower, 41–54.

Mackenzie, A. (2002) Learning at Work: the CLIP experience, *SCONUL Newsletter*, **25** (Spring), 15–17.

Marchington, M. and Wilkinson, A. (2002) *People Management and Development: human resource management at work*, 2nd edn, London, Chartered Institute of Personnel and Development.

Murray, A. and Oldroyd, M. (eds) (2002) *Working Papers on Staff Development Policies*, London, Society of College, National and University Libraries.

Norry, J. (2003) Training for support staff. E-mail to Jo Webb (jwebb@dmu.ac.uk) 11 July 2003.

Ollerenshaw, H. (2001) Library Assistants Seeking Professional Status: who pays and who benefits? *New Review of Information and Library Research*, **7**, 157–85.

Open University. Information Literacy Unit, library.open.ac.uk/help/infolitunit.html.

Oyston, E. (ed.) (2003) *Centred on Learning: academic case studies on learning centre development*, Aldershot, Gower.

Parker, S., Hare, C. and Gannon-Leary, P. (1999) *INSIST: the impact of NVQs in Information and Library Services on staff induction and staff training*, Library and Information Commission Research Report 6, London, Library and Information Commission.

Russell, N. (1985) Professional and Non-professional in Libraries: the need for a new relationship, *Journal of Librarianship*, **17** (4), 293–310.

Sykes, P. (1996) Staff Development for Library Assistants. In Oldroyd, M. (ed.), *Staff Development in Academic Libraries: present practice and future challenges*, London, Library Association Publishing.

Thapisa, A. (1989) The Burden of Mundane Tasks: library assistants' perception of work, *British Journal of Academic Librarianship*, **4** (3), 137–60.

Thapisa, A. (1991) The Motivation Syndrome: job satisfaction through the pay nexus, *International Library Review*, **2**, 141–58.

Webb, J. (1990) The Non-professional in the Academic Library: education for paraprofessionalism, *Personnel, Training and Education*, **7** (2), 21–30.

Whetherly, J. (1998) *Achieving Change through Training and Development*, London, Library Association Publishing.

Winkworth, F. et al. (1999) The Impact of National Vocation Qualifications on Library and Information Services, *Library and Information Briefings*, **86** (June).

Yeatts, D. and Hyten, C. (1998) *High-performing Self-managed Work Teams: a comparison of theory to practice*, Thousand Oaks, Sage.

Young, G. (2003) CLIP. E-mail to Jo Webb (jwebb@dmu.ac.uk) 11 July 2003.

7

Lifelong learning at work: staff development for the flexible workforce

Sue White and Margaret Weaver

Introduction

Academic libraries in the UK and elsewhere are responding to the needs of the next generation of users by extending access to their services – both physically and remotely. Just as the widening of the entry gate into further and higher education has resulted in an upsurge of 'non traditional' students, so the LIS workforce has similarly diversified to deliver hybrid library services, able to anticipate round-the-clock demands.

At the same time, employees are increasingly looking for a more flexible approach to work, which allows them to maintain their desired work–life balance. If libraries are to continue to recruit and retain high calibre staff, managers must be prepared to offer flexibility in working arrangements.

To cope with these developments within (often) declining resources, library and information services (LIS) managers in the UK are employing a variety of staffing models, which incorporate more part-time, fixed-term and flexible working. This chapter offers definitions of flexible work and makes the case for the importance of a coherent and comprehensive approach to training and developing flexible workers including a summary of relevant legislation. Strategies for meeting the challenge of training the flexible workforce are reviewed and a strong case is made for the application of the lifelong learning principle to these vital members of the academic library workforce.

Definitions of flexible work

In the context of this chapter we define these models as posts that have a non-standard work pattern or contract, are temporary in nature, or that have fluid working practices, or are any combination of these patterns.

Goulding and Kerslake's study (1996) is unsurpassed for its in-depth analysis of training flexible information workers. It included the following categories of staff:

- those who work part-time permanently (note there is no standard definition of part-time work; in the UK it is defined by the government as working fewer than 30 hours a week; the European Council Directive on part-time work defines it as someone who is contracted to work fewer than the basic contractual hours of a full-time comparable worker (Chartered Institute of Library and Information Professionals, 2002–3)
- those who job share: where two or more people voluntarily agree to share the responsibilities of the same full-time job
- those who are on full-time or part-time temporary or casual contracts: they are employed on daily, weekly, monthly or other short-term contracts, which end at the employers' discretion
- those who work term-time only to fit in with the teaching weeks of the institution.

The following categories of flexible worker are not covered specifically by the above study but are defined by CILIP (2002–3):

- staff who work annualized hours: a contracted number of hours per year at variable times to suit the needs of the organization

- staff who work compressed hours: employees work more hours per day than is standard within a week or fortnight in exchange for a reduction in the number of working days in that period
- agency staff: casually employed staff who work varying hours to fit in with service priorities or projects, usually at short notice
- student helpers working part-time: students supporting LIS staff within a variety of contexts, for example shelving, giving help and advice, carrying out project work
- staff on flexitime schemes: a system that allows employees to vary their working hours outside agreed core hours but within specific timeframes (similar to staggered hours, which are agreed for individuals allowing for their personal circumstances)
- homeworking: where employees use their home as a work base and carry out all or a part of their work there rather than on employers' premises.

In addition, some posts may have an out-of-hours requirement, whereby some method of call-out is used to maintain essential services and connectivity.

Context

LIS managers have always used flexible staffing arrangements such as those in the first category (above) to maintain long opening hours. However, the compressed hours category shows the changing nature of LIS. In 1996 flexible workers accounted for 40% of all workers in the LIS sector, but a straw poll of ten institutions undertaken by the authors in 2003 suggests that this figure has increased to nearly 50%. However, 'evidence suggests that little thought has been given to the management challenges that accompany an increase in the numbers of flexible workers' (Goulding and Kerslake, 1997, 261). Training and developing staff effectively is one such challenge.

The importance of training for flexible workers

Training is the main way to ensure that services are of a high quality and of a consistent standard. In the 24/7 service environment, this is particularly difficult to achieve because staff may never meet some colleagues who work extended or unsocial hours. Continuity, especially when staff are members of multiple teams, is crucial. Effective staff development helps staff to be better equipped to cope with these situations, deal with the effects of change and use their initiative beyond their immediate job role. Flexible workers require this skill even more than their full-time counterparts.

There are other sound business reasons why LIS managers need to take a proactive stance to developing their flexible workforce. These include legal obligations, workforce planning and performance management, and technology issues.

Legal obligations

Entitlement to access to training opportunities is embodied in various UK and European primary and secondary legislation dealing with employment rights. This is a complex area and there is not space to develop it fully here. The following is a synopsis of the main pieces of legislation affecting flexible workers and training.

The Part-time Workers (Prevention of Less Favourable Treatment) Regulations 2000 (SI 2000 No. 1551) (7) and The Part-time Workers (Prevention of Less Favourable Treatment) (Amendment) Regulations 2002 (SI 2002 No. 2035)

Under these regulations, which first came into force on 1 July 2000, there is an obligation on employers not to exclude part-timers from training and career development. The aim is to ensure that part-time workers are treated *no less favourably* than comparable full-timers, unless different treatment can be objectively justified. Training should be scheduled so that as far as possible staff, including part-timers, can attend. The principle of pro-rata applies and in order to claim that discrimination has taken place, part-timers have to identify a full-timer (either permanent or fixed term) who is receiving more favourable treatment.

The Fixed-term Employees (Prevention of Less Favourable Treatment) Regulations 2002 (SI 2002 No. 2034)

These regulations implement the European Directive on Fixed-Term Work and came into force on 1 October 2002. As with the PTW Regulations above, fixed-term employees should not be treated less favourably than similar permanent employees – and this applies to training.

From 6 April 2003, parents of children aged under six or of disabled children aged under 18 have the right to apply to work flexibly providing they have the qualifying length of service. Employers have a statutory duty to consider their applications seriously.

Disability Discrimination Act 1995 and Special Educational Needs and Disability Act 2001

Employers must not discriminate against an employee (whether they are actually employed or could be employed in the future) with a disability or someone who has had a disability in the past. This includes ensuring that the employer's actions do not put a disabled person at a disadvantage compared with a person without a disability. This also includes promotion opportunities and training (CompactLaw, n.d.). Adjustments must be made to ensure that disabled employees are able to access and take part in training activities.

Sex Discrimination Act 1975

Employees should not be discriminated against on the grounds of their gender or because they are married (CompactLaw, n.d.). This covers opportunities for promotion or training, or both. As a higher percentage of flexible workers are female, managers need to be careful that current practices do not amount to indirect discrimination, for example practices that appear to apply to everyone but which actually discriminate against workers on the grounds of gender.

Race Relations Act 1976

The 1976 Act as amended by the Race Relations (Amendment) Act 2000 imposes a general duty on public bodies to promote equality of opportunity and good race relations (CRE, n.d.). It covers all aspects of employment including training.

Proposed legislation 2003–6

As part of the government agenda on equality and diversity in the workplace, and implementing the European Race and Employment Directives, a raft of legislative measures is planned covering training and trainers (DTI, n.d.). These are at various stages of development and they focus on making sure that workers are not treated unfairly in training situations because of:

- race: amendments to existing Race Relations Act during 2003
- disability: changes to the existing disability legislation by 2004
- age: new law by 2006
- religion: new law during 2003
- being gay or lesbian: new law during 2003.

Workforce planning and performance management

The government's policy is to increase the number of 'family friendly' employers, widen the choice available for parents wishing to combine work and carer responsibilities, and allow people to integrate work and citizenship (DTI, 2003). This is likely to mean that there will be a significant growth in the number of employee-led demands for flexible working. Also, as experienced staff leave, skills and expertise will inevitably be lost; institutions should prepare for this by having succession plans to ensure that gaps do not develop. A systematic training programme, linked to appraisal and performance review, can mitigate the effects. Potentially, however, it can be more difficult for flexible workers to attain the same levels of performance as their full-time counterparts because of their part-time or fragmented working patterns.

Technology

The speed of change in the higher education environment places demands on job roles at all levels. In particular, new learning and teaching methods, and the provision of electronic information, require staff to be competent and confident ICT users. The need for information technology skills and those needed to support changing roles was recognised by the IMPEL2 Project in 1997. It stressed the importance of inclusivity with staff development being 'accessible to all staff who need it' including part-time staff (IMPEL2 Project, 1997). Despite this project's findings and the work of Goulding and Kerslake, there has been little profession-wide debate on the particular needs of flexible workers.

Skills needed by the flexible workforce of the future

To some extent, flexible workers have the same requirements as full-time workers. However, they have some particular needs, which are linked to their patterns of work, their presence at work, their level of supervision (for example staff who work unsocial hours may be supervised less) and the nature of the work itself (for example staff working on innovative short-term development projects may have to deal with a heightened level of uncertainty). An awareness of these needs should help managers to introduce appropriate training strategies.

It is helpful if flexible workers have skills in the following areas:

- responsiveness to change and change management
- ICT, to support remote working

- teamwork and communication, especially for staff working in isolation or in fragmented teams
- time management and personal organization
- keeping up to date with internal and external developments, especially in cases where flexible workers are distanced from mainstream activity
- reflective practice, to promote continuous improvement and engage flexible workers in service development
- knowledge management, this is particularly the case for fixed-term and project team members, so they make sure that project learning is embedded into service improvement.

Managing staff development and training for flexible workers

There are many possible strategies for meeting the various challenges described above, and each institution will adopt the ones best suited to its own particular circumstances.

Organizational culture

First and foremost, flexible workers should be valued as much as their permanent full-time counterparts. It should not be assumed that they are less committed to the organization, or less interested in staff development, just because they work part-time or are on fixed-term contracts.

A culture of training for all should be embraced, which is accepted by everyone in the organization from the most senior managers down. Working towards and maintaining national standards such as Investors in People (IiP) or Charter Mark, whether at an organizational or departmental level, will help engender a commitment to lifelong learning and to valuing the contribution made by all staff.

The development of human resources strategies that embody the principle of equal opportunities is also crucial, and has been encouraged by recent injections of government funding such as the HEFCE Rewarding and Developing Staff initiative.

Training strategy

The development of a LIS training strategy, which sets out the training rights of all employees, is particularly important for flexible workers (Goulding and Kerslake, 1996, 226). The strategy should make transparent the degree of support the organization is prepared to offer, and should encompass staff at all levels and on all types of contract. In devising such a strategy many issues will be raised. For example, when budgets are limited whose staff development needs take priority? Some organizations give all part-time staff a pro-rata entitlement, but even here, flexibility is needed. There may be instances, as in job-share arrangements, where two part-time staff need the same amount of training as a full-time member of staff.

It may help to distinguish between different types of staff development, such as essential on-the-job training (which would include training in operation of new systems and procedures, and to which all staff should be entitled) and non-essential developmental training (which would be subject to negotiation with line managers and to the resources available). Casual workers, agency workers and some fixed-term contract staff would probably qualify for the former but not the latter.

Any LIS training strategy should complement the institution's policy. Tension between central staff development units and in-service activities should be avoided, because what is required is a combination of the two. Flexible workers should be able to take advantage of centrally provided training where appropriate, for example ICT skills and health and safety training. They will also benefit from tailored, locally delivered in-service training, which can be customized to the needs of the service at times to suit the employee. LIS managers should liaise with central units to ensure awareness of the requirements of part-time and flexible workers, and to encourage a flexible approach to delivery. Joint planning of events and programmes avoids duplication of resources, and can be particularly effective for generic skills training such as customer care.

Collaborative training with other local organizations can increase the range of training opportunities open to flexible workers. Several established consortia already exist, offering cross-sector training to LIS workers (for example the M25 Consortium of Higher Education Libraries, and SINTO, the Sheffield Information Organisation). One of the objectives of the recently established regional Museums, Libraries and Archives Councils is to extend training opportunities to a cross-domain audience.

Induction

All staff should be entitled to an induction programme. Where the organization provides its own generic induction, LIS should put pressure on the providers to cater for part-time and flexible workers, for example by offering a modular programme, which can be followed in small chunks rather than requiring attendance for full days. Library induction for flexible workers should be customized to the individual, and there is a strong case for using a simple diagnostic tool to assess particular training needs. For example, people returning to part-time work after a career break might benefit from extra support with time management or ICT training.

The role of line managers

The role of line managers is critical in helping to identify training needs, in encouraging team members to participate in training, and to ensure that training is put into practice afterwards. Giving staff the time to practise what they have learned is even more important for flexible workers who have less time at work to consolidate their training. A full-time assistant who has attended a workshop on word processing will probably be able to find a few hours in ensuing weeks to put their new-found skills into practice. This is much more difficult for a part-timer and line managers need to be aware of this.

Managers should also consider whether their expectations of flexible workers are realistic. The current rate of change brings with it a real danger of overloading part-time staff with too much information or expecting them to undertake too many new duties. There is a limit to the amount of multi-skilling a part-time support assistant can cope with!

All staff, regardless of type of contract, should be entitled to an annual staff development review, ideally supplemented throughout the year with brief discussions between line manager and individual. Organizational policy will dictate whether this review forms part of a broader appraisal system, or is confined to staff development. Flexible workers will particularly benefit from this opportunity to sit down with their line manager, as there may be few such opportunities in the course of the year. All reasonable efforts should be made to ensure these meetings take place, for example by offering flexible workers extra payment to come to work outside their normal working hours, or by the line manager working at non-standard times.

Where possible, flexible workers should be encouraged to participate in activities beyond the confines of their job, for example in LIS committees or cross-team working parties. Involvement in groups is an important component of CPD, offering the opportunity to improve not only technical knowledge, but also generic skills such as working in groups and managing meetings. Flexible workers, and indeed all LIS staff, sometimes need reminding that staff development takes many forms. Reading a journal article, job shadowing a colleague, or participation in a working party is just as valuable as attending a formal course or workshop. The options that are available to staff, and particularly to flexible workers, need to be clearly articulated.

Motivation and incentives

Motivating some staff to undertake development and training is difficult. There are reluctant learners among all categories of staff, and there are many reasons why staff may be disinclined to develop new skills. Flexible workers may not want, or be able, to work extra hours in order to undertake staff training. They may take the view that just 'doing the job' is enough, and they may not see the need to develop themselves. This view is understandable, but could ultimately damage the quality of service delivery through having inadequately trained staff.

The satisfaction of working towards and achieving a recognizable qualification can be a significant incentive. National qualifications include the more established ILS NVQs, the Information and Library Services Progression Award, and the Library and Information Assistants scheme. Increasing numbers of regional schemes are also being established, for example the certificated courses (CLIP and CILS) described in the last chapter. The advantage for flexible workers of many of these schemes is that they are, to a greater or lesser degree, work-based, thus minimizing class contact and travel time.

A further option might be to set up an internal CPD award for support staff. The University of Huddersfield is currently piloting a CPD scheme that offers certification for staff development, on demonstration that work-based learning and reflective practice has taken place.

Continuous improvement targets can serve to motivate and focus performance, providing the targets are both challenging and achievable. Organizations that do not have a culture of appraisal or target setting, may find that introducing targets at team, rather than individual, level may be more motivating in the first instance. Team targets encourage a common purpose and an unwillingness to let the side down.

Communication

Most flexible workers tend to have less time at work than their full-time counterparts. Managers therefore face a significant challenge in ensuring that flexible workers are aware of what is happening in the organization, and feel able to participate in its activities and development.

One strategy to overcome this could be to assign all flexible workers a mentor or 'buddy', whose responsibility is to pass on relevant news or information about changes that have taken place and new initiatives on the horizon. Many organizations assign mentors in the first few months of a new appointment but this could be extended to be a permanent arrangement for flexible workers. The mentor would effectively be taking some of the load off the line manager, who – particularly if they manage a large team – may not be able to devote much time to each team member.

Flexible workers who normally work in off-peak hours such as evenings and weekends could be contractually required to attend training sessions during core hours in the week. Besides being available to undertake essential training, this would have the added benefit of providing networking opportunities with weekday colleagues.

A regular departmental newsletter is a simple device that can be invaluable in keeping all staff up to date with the latest library news. Ideally, it should be sent to the home addresses of term-time-only staff during vacations in order that they keep up to date. There are many examples of newsletters across the HE library sector, and they tend to include a mixture of the latest service developments, changes in staffing, key decisions from committee meetings, advance notice of training courses and light-hearted gossip. They are extremely useful for providing information in easily digestible form, which obviates the need for flexible workers to read the full version of lengthy documents. Especially successful are the models where library staff take ownership of the newsletter and where it is not perceived as a management tool. Part-time staff should be strongly encouraged to contribute articles.

Information about training and staff development events should be readily available to flexible workers, either through the newsletter, a central e-mail system, notice boards, or cascaded via the line manager. Flexible workers need plenty of advance warning of forthcoming activities so they can make alternative domestic arrangements.

Ideally a detailed LIS training programme with course titles and dates should be made available to all staff several months in advance.

Flexible delivery of training

Flexible workers need flexible training, in terms of when, where and how it is delivered. In-house training sessions should be repeated at different times of the day and week, including evenings and weekends if possible. Off-the-job training is more expensive for flexible workers who require time in lieu or overtime payments, but managers must accept this. Flexitime schemes can offer a cheaper alternative, through staff being able to vary their hours of work to attend training.

Where face-to-face training is not essential, alternative forms of training can be considered, for example video recordings of in-house sessions or self-guided commercial products on generic skills such as customer care and managing staff; VLEs can be used to enable access to distance learning materials. The acquisition and development of ICT skills is now an ongoing requirement for LIS staff, and there are excellent web-based tools avilable, such as Netskills and the Resource Discovery Network (RDN) Virtual Training Suite.

Some organizations offer a 'training hour' each week for all staff, where frontline service points are closed but customers have access to self-service facilities. A fixed training hour is not especially helpful to flexible workers, but the increasing use of self-service facilities and custodial opening offer more opportunities for frontline staff to 'close' service points and undertake staff training at off-peak hours.

Cascade training can be an effective way of passing on new skills, and particularly applicable to flexible workers. Rather than an entire weekend team having to come in for training on a new system upgrade during the week, a single member of that team could receive the training, and then pass on their knowledge to colleagues at a convenient time over the weekend. A 'training the trainers' programme may be required to ensure maximum effectiveness.

Conclusion

Linking learning to the workplace role has distinct advantages for the organization and the individual because learning at work and through work enables continuous improvement. Lifelong learning is not just the prerogative of our students, it has to be embedded in working practices and become the norm (Allan, 1999). In the past, flexible workers have not always received the training and development they required, but given the continuing diversification and extension of LIS, managers will be increasingly reliant on flexible workers to provide high quality services over long hours. The agile academic library will be able to move swiftly to meet the changing needs of its customers through a highly trained and effective flexible workforce.

References

Allan, B. (1999) *Developing Information and Library Staff through Workbased Learning*, London, Library Association Publishing.

Chartered Institute of Library and Information Professionals (2002–3) *Flexible Working – the Work-life Balance*, www.cilip.org.uk/jobs_careers/flexible.html.

Commission for Racial Equality, www.cre.gov.uk/legaladv/rra.html.

CompactLaw, www.compactlaw.co.uk/dda95.html.

Department of Trade and Industry, www.dti.gov.uk/er/equality/ldconsult.pdf.

Department of Trade and Industry. (2003) *Balancing Work and Family Life: enhancing choice and support for parents*, www.dti.gov.uk/er/individual/balancing.pdf.

Disability Discrimination Act 1995, Chapter 50, HMSO, www.legislation.hmso.gov.uk/.

The Fixed-Term Employees (Prevention of Less Favourable Treatment) Regulations 2002 (SI 2002 No. 2034), HMSO, www.legislation.hmso.gov.uk/.

Goulding, A. and Kerslake, E. (1996) *Developing the Flexible Library and Information Workforce: a quality and equal opportunities perspective*, London, British Library Research and Innovation Centre.

Goulding, A. and Kerslake, E. (1997) Training the Flexible Library and Information Workforce: problems and practical solutions, *Information Services and Use*, **17**(4), 61.

IMPEL2 Project (1997) IMPEL2 Project: an eLib Project funded by the JISC, http://online.northumbria.ac.uk/faculties/art/information_studies/impel/.

The Part-time Workers (Prevention of Less Favourable Treatment) Regulations 2000 (SI 2000 No. 1551), HMSO, www.legislation.hmso.gov.uk/.

The Part-time Workers (Prevention of Less Favourable Treatment) (Amendment) Regulations 2002 (SI 2002 No. 2035), HMSO, www.legislation.hmso.gov.uk/.

Race Relations Act 1976, Chapter 74, London, HMSO.

Sex Discrimination Act 1975, Chapter 65, London, HMSO.

Special Educational Needs and Disability Act 2001, Chapter 10, London, HMSO, www.legislation.hmso.gov.uk/.

8

Delivering staff development using a virtual learning environment

Moira Bent

A key characteristic of the learning organization is the ability of its members to find or make opportunities to learn (Noriaka and Takeuchi, 1995).

Introduction

The last five years have seen a rapid growth in the use of virtual learning environments (VLEs) in higher education in the UK. E-learning and e-skills are also commonly used terms. Staff at all levels in academic libraries are working in an environment that demands constant updating of their skills. Among a plethora of e-skills, library staff are now required to understand what VLEs are, answer questions and understand their applications and use them in teaching information literacy skills to students. It could be thought that this latter skill might be required by a small number of subject staff only, but students expect that library staff at all levels have an understanding of the educational environment in which they work, and often fail to distinguish between different levels of staff at information points. In fact, students interact more frequently with support staff than with senior staff, and investment in VLE training at all levels is important.

Libraries are also opening for longer hours than in the past, so 'staff development managers are faced with the additional challenge of delivering staff training and development opportunities that are equally accessible to all staff regardless of the hours they work, or where they work' (Dale, 2002).

This chapter will consider the implications of using a VLE as part of a library staff development programme, drawing on experiences at Newcastle University Library.

Definitions

It may be helpful to start with some definitions:

- *E-Learning*: E-learning is learning that is delivered, enabled or mediated by electronic technology for the explicit purpose of training and/or education (Allan, 2002). It can include a wide range of activities such as interactive web-based packages and electronic communication.
- *Managed learning environment (MLE)*: An MLE is a system that uses technology to enhance and make more effective the network of relationships between learners, teachers and organizers of learning through integrated support for richer communications and activities. A modern university is an example of a managed learning environment in the broadest sense, though it is more often taken to mean the software that links the various systems in the university together.
- *Virtual learning environments (VLE)*: A VLE is a software package that supports online or e-learning; it consists of components in which tutors and learners participate in online interactions. It provides a focus for learning activities, their management and facilitation, along with the provision of content and resources. A useful diagram of how a VLE integrates with a managed learning environment was circulated by the British Educational Communications and Technology Agency (BECTA, 1999) and has been

reproduced by the Joint Information Systems Council (JISC, 2002); see Figure 8.1.

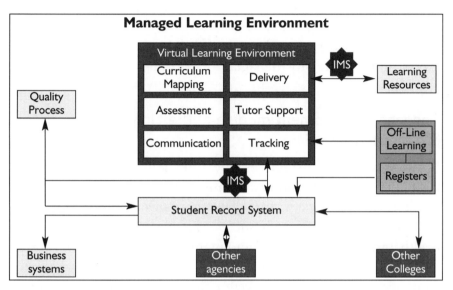

Figure 8.1   Example of how a VLE integrates with an MLE (diagram by Bob Powell, © BECTA)

There are many different VLE packages on the market; perhaps the most commonly used ones in the UK at present are Blackboard and WebCT, but others include Lotus Learning Space, COSE and Learning Landscapes (see reference list for details).

Using a VLE for staff development

Using a VLE as a training medium has the dual benefit of delivering training via the VLE and at the same time enabling library staff to develop practical skills in the use and understanding of the VLE. This means that they will be better equipped to understand the problems students encounter while using the interface, and will be familiar enough with the environment to understand its potential for library use. The JISC recommends that institutions should 'where possible use the VLE software to provide staff training as it will encourage staff to reflect on the learning experience of using a VLE'

(JISC, 2001). Although referring to the training of academic staff in the use of a VLE, this statement applies equally to the training of library staff. Interestingly, this document includes a table of the VLE skills that it recommends various groups of university staff should have, and it appears that library staff need more skills than anyone except senior university managers!

The staff development module at the University of Newcastle upon Tyne

Building on these principles, the staff development module at Newcastle University Library was introduced in January 2002 using Blackboard. It covers a wide range of topic areas, ranging from using the world wide web, specific subject skills, personal skills, IT skills, health and safety, 'hot topics' and many more (Bent, 2002). All staff in the library are registered on the staff development module as students and can access the materials either in timetabled staff training time or in free time at home or at work. Staff who are involved in delivering any kind of training to their colleagues become 'course builders' and are encouraged to add their own training materials and documentation to the module.

Within each section of the module the materials have been split into training resources – material that can be worked through, such as workbooks and quizzes, and background documentation – a way of using Blackboard as a central, easily accessible repository for manuals and guides. See Figure 8.2.

All staff have been introduced to the module in a library-wide demonstration and have been provided with simple logon instructions. Guidelines have been developed for course builders to ensure that consistency is maintained and that they are all given individual training in mounting resources onto the system as needed.

This approach is very different from the use of a VLE in the curriculum. Rather than delivering a whole structured course, Newcastle University Library is offering a series of 'bites'. Staff do not need to follow the materials through in one logical route, they can pick and

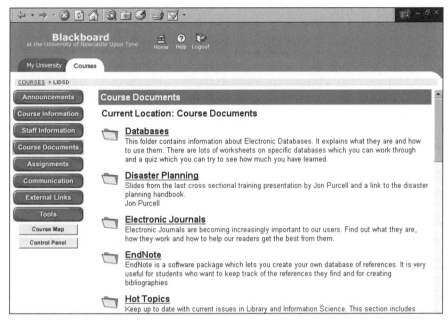

Figure 8.2   An example of the use of Blackboard to provide a VLE at the University of Newcastle upon Tyne

choose to meet their own personal needs. The module allows a 'just in time' approach to staff development. Using a VLE in this way involves close consultation with the technical support team in the institution. In a 'normal' academic module, students move on at the end of the year and the module is recycled. This is inappropriate for a staff development module, on which staff may be registered as students for several years. Specific arrangements may need to be made with the learning technology team to avoid loss of students and their associated assessment marks at year-end roll-over time. So far, no formal evaluation has been made of this pilot project, although informal feedback from individual library staff is positive. The library management has yet to make a decision on the future of the pilot project.

The staff development module at Edge Hill College

In contrast, a staff development module has been developed at Edge Hill College of Higher Education in which staff follow through a structured module on a topic such as information literacy. Staff at Edge Hill are operating in a converged service, offering support for users of WebCT, and staff and students at the college have an expectation that support will be provided (Martin and McLoughlin, 2003). IT and information needs of information and media services staff are assessed either on appointment or via appraisal, and staff follow a comprehensive induction programme called ProVIDE. The European Computer Driving Licence is available, as well as a four-week course about supporting online learning, which is delivered as blended learning, with face-to-face workshops backed up by online materials. Feedback is obtained via group discussion with participants and has been very positive. Staff like the content and design of the module, but admit to preferring face-to-face interactions and to having problems of time management.

Benefits of using a VLE for staff development

A VLE offers a new dimension to training and development opportunities. It should not be seen as an alternative method of training, but rather as an additional support to an existing programme. It allows staff to build up their expertise using technology that is freely available in the university and in general less technical support is needed (Minshull, 2001).

Flexibility

Online learning can be extremely flexible for trainers. New material can be integrated seamlessly and errors rectified quickly. It can be an economic method of delivering training as online materials are cheaper to deliver than print. It can be scaled up and it is efficient in delivery (Milligan, 1999). The approach also enables standardization of training; it brings together a lot of different teachers' materials and the individual trainers can learn from each other in terms of delivery and creation of materials so that the overall quality of training improves. This allows peer learning for trainers, a side of staff development that is often missing! Opportunities for collaboration between libraries in different institutions mean that staff can share good practice and save time in developing resources. Many staff training and development materials have a generic core so it can be time saving to have a central resource, which can then be tailored for specific applications or libraries.

This approach is being demonstrated by the LiLo project, in which staff training resources are being developed collaboratively between the university libraries of Durham and Newcastle upon Tyne (Purcell and Bent, 2003). LiLo will produce a module of teaching-related materials using Blackboard, materials that embed the practical aspects of library work into the theory of teaching and learning, offering a blended learning experience for library staff. The work is based on existing collaborative workshops, which give library staff skills to help them teach users how to find information. If successful, the resources will be made available to all academic library staff in north-east England. Figure 8.3 illustrates the introductory page of the LiLo module at the University of Newcastle upon Tyne.

For learners, the delivery of staff training using a VLE offers the opportunity to learn what a VLE is and how it is used in learning. 'The experience of using the VLE is in itself a learning experience' (FERL, 2003). It gives staff the freedom to customize their own learning experience and to follow their individual paths through the same learning materials. Part-time staff, or staff who work unsocial hours, can be included in training activities within their work time, rather than having to reorganize their schedules to accommodate training sessions. Staff who work at remote locations, perhaps in small departmental libraries, who often are unable to attend training owing to small staff numbers, are also able to participate fully. This helps to reinforce the inclusion of all staff and combat any feelings of isolation.

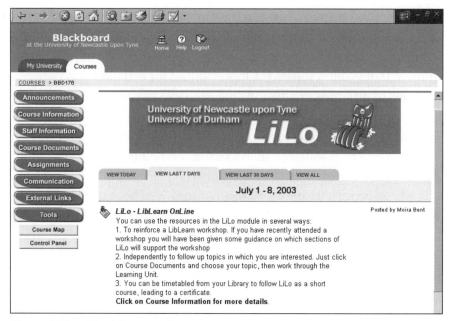

Figure 8.3   The LiLo module

Staff who are motivated to do so have the opportunity to extend their development beyond the normal training activities without impinging on their normal work. Learning about library issues can often be tedious and an important benefit of this interface is that it can make learning fun and attractive to less motivated staff. Quizzes are usually popular and give learners instant feedback, while the survey function provides instant feedback to trainers on the success of their material.

A VLE can be a great leveller. Everyone approaches the material on equal terms, whatever their position in the library hierarchy, and staff who feel intimidated in a face-to-face training session may feel more confident about participating in a virtual environment as a VLE is usually a non-threatening space. Self-paced learning is possible as staff also have the opportunity to revisit the resource at their leisure, thus reinforcing the learning process. It should be realized, however, that everyone has different learning styles and this approach to learning will inevitably appeal more to some staff than others. In practice, staff will need to be very motivated to give up leisure time to look at the resources!

Collaboration and integration

The opportunities that a joint staff development module offers for collaboration between libraries mean that staff can exchange experiences and share good practice, just as they would in a more time consuming face-to-face meeting. It is possible to envisage practitioner networks working across libraries allowing for the sharing of good practice and peer learning. The Chartered Institute of Personnel and Development suggests that e-learning in general can offer 'more learning opportunities, more efficiently to more staff' (CIPD, 2002).

It is also possible to use the functionality of the VLE as an intranet for the library and to manage communication within the interface. User groups and communities can be created to manage projects or communicate on specific topics. Discussion fora can be encouraged. The calendar function can be used to keep track of all staff training and development opportunities and staff will always be able to find out what training is available.

It is possible to use a VLE for development purposes as well as for training, so individuals can use it to further their continuing professional development. Links to further material such as Netskills (Netskills, n.d.) can be included, as well as links to web resources of interest. At Newcastle University Library, one section of the VLE explains 'everything you always wanted to know about staff development', including practical issues such as how to fill out forms requesting external courses, links to rail timetables and a copy of the staff development policy. A VLE is also a good opportunity to keep staff up to date with topical issues; links can be made to recent electronic articles and other sites of professional interest. Although a VLE can focus staff on what is available to them, it is difficult for it to be comprehensive.

Assessment and evaluation

The assessment element of a VLE means that the tracking of learning activity is also possible. Staff training managers can monitor which sections of the module are most popular with staff, and even track the progress of individuals if they are following a structured programme. Evaluation of the resources is possible using the survey facility. Once the module has been set up and embedded into the library culture, it can prove useful for the induction of new members of staff. Induction is traditionally a time-consuming process for existing staff and the VLE can provide useful support in terms of giving background information. Provision of a VLE can help to occupy new staff in between face-to-face induction training; exploring aVLE can be a fun and easy way for new recruits to be assimilated into the library, as long as they already have basic IT skills.

There is great potential for materials to be used regionally or even nationally as a way of sharing ideas and resources, as much library staff training has a generic core. Perhaps links can be set up with local departments of library and information studies or bodies such as the Learning and Skills Council in order to have the learning accredited. Accreditation can be a great motivating factor for staff.

Issues to consider in the use of a VLE for staff development

The CIPD survey of the use of e-learning in staff development in the UK discovered that the tendency has been to spend only a small proportion of the staff development budget on e-learning (CIPD 2002). Of the training managers who use e-learning, 50% spend less than 10% of their budget on it. FERL recommends that 'considerable resources must be invested to ensure you get the most from the VLE' (2003). There are obviously many resource implications in the adoption of a VLE for staff training in libraries. Although the VLE itself is usually in use in the institution and is accessible free of charge, staff must still have access to suitable equipment. If the staff development module is truly meant to be equally accessible for all staff, from shelvers to the chief librarian, then all staff must be able to gain access to a PC at a convenient time. This may mean that a dedicated training space must be provided, such as the staff training room at Newcastle University Library, or that attention must be given to the use of PCs within working areas. All staff should feel that they have equal access to a PC for training purposes.

The time that trainers need to invest in the creation of the learning materials should be recognized as another resource issue. It is easy to underestimate the conceptual leap required to use a VLE effectively; trainers may need to rethink the learning process and how it works in this new environment. Existing training materials cannot just be copied into a module and expected to work. This concept may be difficult to get across to existing library trainers and, once it is realized, it can be a daunting prospect to translate resources from teaching into learning materials. Teachers and trainers may need investment in their skills to enable them to achieve this successfully. As well as pedagogical skills, staff developers may need highly developed IT skills to enable them to create exciting, interactive learning materials. Littlejohn and Lorna (2003) feel that many staff developers have a poorly developed base for online teaching and lack experience of software such as web-page software and screen capture techniques.

Participation in a VLE at even the most fundamental level requires some basic IT skills and it is important to establish how far these skills are embedded within the existing staff. An immediate barrier is encountered if staff are not familiar or confident with IT and this can lead to a bad first impression if displayed publicly, which will be difficult to counteract later. Therefore, resources may also need to be invested in upskilling all staff to having a basic level of IT competence. In the current climate in education, this can only be a helpful development.

Expectations are important – what does the library management expect from the staff and what do staff expect from their staff development programme? Do we want our staff to be self-directed, independent learners? This may involve a shift in our perception of staff development and our roles within it. To what extent does the existing staff development policy need to be redrafted to accommodate the use of a VLE? Does the staff development policy specify learning outcomes for staff which can be translated into an online environment? How can the management of a staff development module in a VLE be administered? Who will be responsible for maintaining and updating it? All these questions need to be addressed if such a project is to be successful.

E-learning can be viewed as a radical innovation and it requires a new attitude to learning on behalf of the learners. It can be perceived as off-putting and impersonal, or difficult to understand. If staff are happy with the present training scene there is little incentive for them to change. Akerlind (Akerlind and Trevitt, 1999) explains that staff have a built-in resistance to change, that we must expect it and not be discouraged by it, as trying something new typically produces feelings of discomfort and anxiety. It is the role of senior managers in the library to encourage staff to participate in the VLE, as it will only be effective with commitment from the top, bottom and all levels in between.

The attitude of the library management team is indeed vital to the success of a staff development VLE. The value of the VLE needs to be embedded in the culture of the library at all levels and its use encouraged daily by line managers. It may be helpful to have 'champions' in each section of the library – staff who have a little more experience of the VLE than their colleagues and can help with the development of training resources and use of materials. Again, there may be training and resource implications. Library staff should be encouraged to use the VLE as part of their daily work, perhaps by using it for staff newsletters, advertising social events or even as a swap shop for personal items for sale. The module must be easily accessible from the desktop.

In considering the adoption of a VLE for staff training and development, the library has to make a fundamental decision about the future direction of its staff training policy. Is online learning a satisfactory substitute for face-to-face learning? The benefits of informal contact in learning at work must not be underestimated. Looking at the staff training programme as a whole, it may be possible to identify activities that lend themselves better to a VLE than to a more traditional training medium. The CIPD survey found that at the time of the survey e-learning was used more for practical skills such as IT and less for soft skills such as communication and team building (CIPD, 2002). Library managers may decide that the VLE is only appropriate for certain types of learning or even for certain levels of staff. For example, senior staff may have jobs that allow them sufficient freedom to participate in online discussions, while support staff may be rigidly timetabled and find involvement in this activity more difficult. If they decide that they want all staff to be involved, then they must make a conscious effort to have a structure or environment in the library that supports this, perhaps using mechanistic methods such as training hours. They must be prepared to enable the transition process or any potential educational success will be limited.

Conclusion

'Any new innovation in staff development must have an advantage over existing provision and must be consistent with the needs of the organization' (Rogers, 1995). Although VLEs are new and can be seen as an exciting way to transform staff development, library managers must be sure, as Rogers says, that their use will improve the current staff training programme.

A critical benefit of staff development comes from sharing experiences with others and sometimes face-to-face training is the only way to do that. However, use of a VLE will allow staff whose circumstances do not permit them to attend training sessions to at least gain some benefit from interaction with their colleagues. Libraries employ staff of all levels and abilities. Organized training will often lead to them being grouped with their peers, with no opportunities for them to broaden their horizons, widen awareness, or pursue individual interests. To what extent do library managers (and all senior library staff) have a responsibility for the general development of their staff, as opposed to training them to do the job? Providing resources via a VLE for motivated staff is one way of meeting this need. 'If a company is a learning organization it provides an environment in which self directed learning will flourish' (Confessore and Cops, 1998).

A VLE should be only one tool in an integrated staff development programme, part of a blended learning experience for library staff. The decision to use a VLE must be justified on the basis of the quality of the learning experience and the suitability of the technology to the learning outcomes (Milligan, 1999). The decision to use a VLE requires commitment from the top to embed it into the culture of the library and 'champions' in different library sections will aid the process. Such commitment also implies that sufficient resources will be invested to develop the new training environment.

However, staff development is an ongoing process, both formal and informal, and it needs to be personalized, tailored and relevant. A VLE offers the chance to develop a package of staff development and training resources that can be used by all library staff in different ways and at different times, thus giving them a much wider range of opportunities.

References:

Akerlind, G. S. T. and Trevitt, A. C. (1999) Enhancing Self-directed Learning through Educational Technology: when students resist the change, *Innovations in Education and Training International*, **36** (2), 96–105.

Allan, B. (2002) *E-learning and Teaching in Library and Information Services*, London, Facet Publishing.

Bent, M. (2002) Blackboard and Staff Development at Newcastle University Library, *SCONUL Newsletter* (25), 13–14.

Blackboard, www.blackboard.com/.

British Educational Communications and Technology Agency (1999) *What is a Managed Learning Environment?*, www.becta.org.uk/.

Chartered Institute of Personnel and Development (2002) *Training and Development 2002: survey report*, London, CIPD, www.cipd.co.uk/.

Confessore, S. J. K. and Cops, W. J. (1998) Self Directed Learning and the Learning Organisation: examining the connection between the individual and the learning environment, *Human Resource Development Quarterly*, **9** (4), 365–75.

Creation of Study Environments, http://web.staffs.ac.uk/COSE/.

Dale, P. (2002) Using Worksheets to Encourage Independent Learning by Staff in an Academic Library: a case study, *Library Management* **23** (8/9), 394–402.

FERL (2003) *Focus on Virtual Learning Environments: staff development*, British Educational Communications and Technology Agency, http://ferl.becta.org.uk/.

Joint Information Systems Council (2001) *Technical Training and Staff Development*, www.jisc.ac.uk/mle/reps/briefings/.

Joint Information Systems Council (2002), *MLEs and VLEs explained*, JISC Briefing Paper no. 1, www.jisc.ac.uk/uploaded_documents/bp1.pdf.

Learning Landscapes, http://toomol.bangor.ac.uk/ll/.

Littlejohn, A. C. and Lorna, M. (2003) From Pilot Project to Strategic Development: scaling up staff support in the use of ICT for teaching and learning, *Journal of Further and Higher Education*, **27** (1), 47–52.

Lotus Learning Space, www.lotus.com/home.nsf/welcome/learnspace/.

Martin, L. and McLoughlin, D. (2003) *Flexible Approaches to E-literacy for Staff in a Converged Service*. Presentation at e-Lit 2003, Glasgow, www.iteu.gla.ac.uk/elit/elit2003/papers/martinl_web.html.

Milligan, C. (1999) *Delivering Staff and Professional Development Using Virtual Learning Environments*, JTAP, JISC Technology

Applications Programme, Heriot-Watt University,
www.jtap.ac.uk/reports/htm/jtap-044.html.

Minshull, G. (2001) *VLE mistakes – how to get it all wrong!*,
Direct Learn Training Ltd, www.directlearn.co.uk.

Netskills Internet Training Service, www.netskills.ac.uk/.

Noriaka, L. and Takeuchi, H. (1995) *The Knowledge Creating
Company*, New York, Oxford University Press.

Purcell, C. and Bent, M. (2003) *LiLo: keeping afloat with staff
development (using a VLE for staff development)*. Presentation
at e-Lit 2003, Glasgow,
www.iteu.gla.ac.uk/elit/elit2003/papers/purcell_web.html.

Rogers, E. M. (1995) *Diffusion of Innovations*, New York, Free
Press.

WebCT, www.webct.com.

9

Collaborative staff development

Philippa Dolphin

Introduction

There is a long history of networking and collaboration between libraries. Partnerships, co-operatives, consortia and networks provide a range of opportunities to extend and improve services and reduce costs. There have been strong library networks in the UK since the 1950s, but their number and power have increased rapidly over the last ten years. Although there are many reasons for this growth, the provision of improved staff development and training opportunities has invariably been an important factor. This chapter will look at staff development offered by UK academic libraries in collaboration and what makes it successful. The focus is on local and regional collaboration rather than on subscription-based national bodies such as the Chartered Institute of Library and Information Professionals (CILIP) and its subgroups, SCONUL, and the Consortium of University Research Libraries (CURL) – all of which have an involvement in staff development.

The development of partnerships

Partnerships such as HATRICS: the Southern Information Network, the Hertfordshire Technical Information Service (HERTIS) and

Birmingham Libraries Cooperative Mechanisation Project (BLCMP), which grew up in the 1950s and 1960s, were usually established with a view to sharing resources locally, working on automation projects or sharing catalogue records. Some of these bodies, for example HERTIS, provided a large programme of courses and visits for staff in member libraries.

The new breed of academic library consortia in the UK was partly stimulated by the increase in student numbers in the 1990s and the pressures on library resources. The Follett Report (Joint Funding Councils' Libraries Review Group, 1993) gave strong backing to the development of local and regional co-operative arrangements between libraries as a means of sharing staff and resource costs. The Review Group visited four metropolitan areas (Edinburgh, Manchester, Newcastle and London) to look at different aspects of inter-library co-operation and networking. They identified five key factors contributing to successful collaboration:

- a clear statement governing the purpose and scope of collaborative arrangements, which forms the basis of agreement between collaborating libraries and institutions
- a clear framework governing the management of co-operative arrangements, to which the staff of each participating institution are committed
- strong support from senior institutional management and academic departments
- collaborative arrangements that take full account of the practical implications for users and staff in each co-operating institution
- the physical proximity of institutions and the convenience of shared use for students and staff.

As a result of the Follett Report funding became available for collaborative projects between higher education libraries, and subsequently with libraries in different sectors. The Labour Government that came to power in 1997 gave further impetus to linking and partnerships within and beyond the sector. National funding through a range of initiatives such as the Research Support Libraries Programme and the New Opportunities Fund has invariably gone to institutions working in collaboration.

The two biggest collaborative providers of staff training and development for academic librarians became established during this period. The Consortium of University Research Libraries in Manchester (CALIM) was set up in 1992 and offered reciprocal access arrangements to students in five closely located universities. The stimulus for the creation of the M25 Consortium of Higher Education Libraries in 1993 was to improve access for students and researchers to the enormous variety and wealth of collections in the London area. Elsewhere in the UK regional consortia have grown up in response to local needs and issues, funding and transport arrangements. Although not all of them have a training and development role, the experience of working with staff from other institutions is in itself valuable staff development. Evans (2002) writing on the benefits of co-operation in the USA highlights this as an important factor: 'one benefit not frequently discussed, is the potential for the improvement in the working relationships among the co-operating libraries ... some systems, finding this to be important, have set up exchange internships for staff members, both professional and para-professional'.

In the USA collaboration has also been an important part of library activity for more than 20 years: 'Collaborative ideas currently have high social and cultural value. Organisations (nation states, college and universities, academic libraries, and funding agencies) extol the virtue of collaboration' (Peters, 2003). But the enormous recent growth has largely been a result of the advent of favourable licence deals for consortial purchase of electronic information. In the UK universities benefit from electronic licence deals negotiated nationally by the Joint Information Systems Committee (JISC). In 2003 there were nearly 160 members of the informal International Coalition of Library Consortia (ICOLC, n.d.) which is largely concerned with sharing information about networked information providers and their pricing practices. But there are many regional groupings, the majority of which include staff development and training among their benefits. A study of collaborative systems in Ohio (Schneider, 2002), for example, indicates that access to continuing education was a major factor in the decision to join the regional system. Respondents to Schneider's survey also stressed that 'regional library systems offered a medium for human networking and a broader understanding of issues facing all libraries, features that were unavailable from other organizations'.

Activity within the UK in 2003

CPD25 – training and development for higher education libraries in the London region

The M25 Consortium of Academic Libraries (www.M25lib.ac.uk/) is the largest regional consortium of libraries in higher education, with 44 members serving a total of 680,000 students and staff in the London region. Staff development in London university libraries went through a period of transition in 2002 when the M25 Staff Development Group and the University of London Staff Training Group merged to form CPD25 – Training and Development for HE Libraries in the London Region (www.cpd25.ac.uk/). The aims of CPD25 are to:

- provide high quality staff development and training for all levels of staff in London's higher education libraries
- provide a range of cost-effective and value-for-money events and activities for all participating libraries
- underpin and facilitate the work plan of the M25 Consortium and the University Libraries' Committee (ULC) by arranging relevant seminars, conferences and other events
- provide opportunities for all levels of HE library staff in London to meet each other
- foster good practice among participating members and facilitate the exchange of experience

- provide an overview of staff development and training issues on behalf of the M25 Consortium and the ULC as required.

Following the establishment of CPD25, the M25 Consortium subscriptions were increased to cover the salary of an administrator to look after training and development publicity, bookings and finances. Increases in subscription levels can often lead to disagreements among consortium members, particularly where these vary considerably in terms of staff numbers, size of budget and mission. It was agreed that the most equitable way to allocate this increase was to base it on full-time equivalent library staff numbers (Joint M25 and University of London Staff Training and Development Group Review, 2002). Events are generally low cost and most visits are free. Higher charges are levied for non-members of the Consortium.

The first year of CPD25 is generally acknowledged to have been a success, although there has been no evaluation of the whole programme. The five factors for successful collaboration identified by the Follett Review Group are certainly present. The existence of a dedicated administrator and good public transport in the London area have been particularly important. By the end of the first year there had been nearly 1,000 participants in events and visits. The programme included the best aspects of the two previous groups: a successful three-day management course run by an external trainer, events for graduate trainees, a Chartership workshop programme, and a large programme of visits to libraries all over London. In addition, 25 major events were available during 2002–3 organized by members of the five task groups, which are responsible for career development, statutory regulation and legal compliance, operations management, personal effectiveness and management, and user resources and services. In many ways the staff development programme serves to knit the Consortium together. About 50 staff are involved in the task groups, staff from all levels take part in events and visits, the variety of venues serves to emphasize the richness of London's collections, and parts of the programme are designed to back up the Consortium business plan. Future plans include online booking and work on benchmarking with an Australian university.

Consortium of University Research Libraries in Manchester

The Consortium of University Research Libraries in Manchester (CALIM, www.calim.ac.uk/) was a smaller, less diverse, but slightly longer established consortium. Members of CALIM were Manchester University, Manchester Business School, Manchester Metropolitan University, Salford University and University of Manchester Institute of Science and Technology (UMIST). The Consortium aimed to increase opportunities, eliminate duplication, improve value for money and improve communication between members through its staff development and training programme (CALIM Staff Training and Development Standing Committee, n.d.). The CALIM programme offered extensive opportunities for professional and personal development to a total of about 600 staff. This resulted in significant savings in costs (Porter, 2001), although subscriptions had to be adequate to cover the costs of central administration, including approximately two staff dedicated to the training and development programme.

CALIM had always worked closely with North West Academic Libraries (NoWAL). There were nine members of NoWAL, all SCONUL members. One of its objectives was to engage in collaborative staff development, and NoWAL members had been able to attend CALIM events at a discounted rate. In August 2002 CALIM joined NoWAL, which now has 15 members in Lancashire, Manchester and Merseyside. All CALIM training and development is subsumed under the leadership of NoWAL, resulting in a considerable enlargement of collaborative staff development in the north west.

The 2002–3 programme includes over 40 events covering library and information issues, personal and professional effectiveness, management and IT skills, plus an annual lecture. The programme is accessible via the web and in a hard copy brochure, together with a booking form and biographical information about trainers and speakers. Staff can also take part in the staff development programmes of each member institution through an agreement between their staff development units.

A particularly ambitious and successful part of the new consortium's training activity is the Certificate in Library and Information Practice (CLIP), which had been developed by CALIM. It is targeted at staff without library and information qualifications, but is open to any member of staff wishing to develop their skills. It was created after a brief audit in 1998, which revealed that very few staff were undertaking formal qualifications. It was decided to investigate the demand for a locally accredited programme aimed at unqualified staff. A training needs analysis revealed that the main demand for training was in the areas of library and information skills, information technology, internet skills, health and safety, customer service and management. Some of these were available at the right level as Open College Network units, but seven new units were authored by the (then) CALIM Staff Development and Training Committee – a learning experience in itself, according to Porter (2001). The majority of tutors for the units worked at CALIM institutions. Individuals have the opportunity to obtain nationally recognized credits or the full Certificate in Library and Information Practice, or both. Staff who have attended courses or built up significant experience may take advantage of accreditation of prior learning (APL). The range of subject areas is changing, and CLIP is being adapted and widened to include learning and teaching. It has involved a substantial investment of time, but Mackenzie (2002) believes it has achieved everything it set out to achieve and more. CLIP and the general programme of courses are open to staff who work outside the consortium's libraries. Jo Webb has commented on CLIP in her earlier chapter about academic library support staff.

Consortium staff wishing to become Chartered Members of CILIP can do so by completing its Standard Professional Training Programme (SPTP). In addition to local training and development, candidates attend a number of courses on presentation skills, team working, communication, finance and professional awareness. These courses are offered either as standalone sessions or as part of the general staff training and development programme.

Other collaborative activity in England

There tend to be examples of co-operative training and development wherever there are clusters of universities and colleges. Bath University, Bath Spa University, Bristol University and the University of the West of England have created Avon University Libraries in Co-operation (AULIC, www.uwe.ac.uk/library/info/ aulic.htm). The AULIC Staff Development Group aims to share staff development information, expertise and good practice and to hold joint conferences, training events and provide other opportunities. The group has been in existence for over ten years and organizes a one-day conference each year, a rolling programme of visits and one-off events concentrating on core skills. It has secured agreement from City of Bristol College to run an NVQ course for library staff. East Midlands Academic Library and Information Services in Co-operation (EMALINK) was established in 1985, largely for the purposes of co-operative staff development. Current members are Bishop Grosseteste College, Coventry, De Montfort, Derby, Leicester, Loughborough, Nottingham, Nottingham Trent, Open and Warwick universities and University College Northampton. Objectives of the group include shared development and training activities including an annual programme of events. Each HEI contributes at least one event per annum to the programme and staff exchanges and visits are facilitated. Events are free to members. There is some skills training, but the group's main focus is on bringing together peer groups and facilitating exchange of experience sessions. An added benefit is the opportunity for steering group members, who are all senior managers, to exchange information and good practice on human resource management issues. In Sunderland, a city now well known for co-operation between libraries, the existing consortium of academic and public library partners received New

Opportunities Funding in 1999 to deliver information and communications technology training via the web for school and public library staff (Sharpe, 2000). There are several other groups, such as Learning through Libraries in Plymouth and the Liverpool Libraries Partnership, which offer small amounts of training and development co-operatively with libraries in the same city or region, often including public and special libraries.

Collaborative activity in Scotland and Wales

There are numerous other examples of collaborative staff development in the UK. Some groupings include national, public or special libraries. The largest groups are in Scotland and Wales, although since both are run by volunteers rather than a secretariat they cannot offer the same number or range of events as the M25 Consortium or NoWAL. The different Scottish higher education system and separate funding and quality arrangements in the home countries are strong drivers here, together with the problems of travel to other parts of the UK. The Scottish Academic Libraries Cooperative Training Group (www.jiscmail.ac.uk/files/LIS-SALCTG/welcome.html) has been in existence since 1986. All 19 higher education libraries in Scotland and two national libraries are members. Two of the group's aims are to identify common training needs and to organize training events to satisfy them, and to work co-operatively to provide training and education in librarianship. The website states that it responds to the training and development requirements of all library staff by presenting a range of courses, both practical and managerial, at excellent value for money. There are six to seven events per year varying from half a day to two days in length. Initiatives being pursued in 2002 included closer liaison with other bodies in the information profession and more formal training for library assistants (Ulas, 2002). A slightly smaller group is the Wales Higher Education Libraries Forum (WHELF, n.d.). Members of WHELF comprise the 13 higher education institutions in Wales. WHELF and HEWIT (the group of IT managers for Welsh higher education institutions) have formed a staff development group, which organizes training events for members and identifies good practice. The annual colloquium held at Gregynog Hall (the University of Wales' conference centre) is particularly successful. There is a lively website with online booking, and presentations are put up after the event.

Collaborative activity in Ireland

Training officers in Irish university libraries had been working together for many years prior to the setting up of the Academic and National Library Training Cooperative (ANLTC, www.anltc.ie/) in 1995. There are 11 members: eight university libraries from the Republic, the national library, and the two universities from Northern Ireland. As there is no central staffing, each participating institution is committed to organizing at least one course. Between 1996 and 2002 over 1,000 participants have attended a total of 68 ANLTC courses and the evaluation results are publicly available on their website. ANLTC now plays a key role in academic library staff development, helping libraries adjust to rapid culture change and service demands in Irish universities (Cox and Fallon, 2002).

Benefits and challenges

Collaborative staff development is obviously very much on the agenda of academic libraries in the UK in the 21st century. In addition to the obvious benefit of enabling the training budget to go further, there are significant savings in travel costs and time. Local networking is improved and any existing consortium work is strengthened. Regional political and social issues are often better addressed within a local staff development context. But staff development via consortia poses many challenges. Who does the work? Decision-making in consortia is very time-consuming and can be inefficient. Innovative and stimulating staff development programmes require input from energetic and determined leaders, but people involved have other priorities and pressures and their first loyalty must be to their own institution. Without dedicated administrative support this kind of staff development cannot expand beyond a certain level. Large consortia cannot run a significant programme through the work of volunteers. However, the employment of a central secretariat necessitates the introduction of, or a major increase in, subscriptions, plus a more formal commitment to collaborative work. This needs delicate handling to ensure that smaller members with fewer staff and lower budgets, or members with distinctive needs and missions, are not disadvantaged and do not sense a loss of control. The organizing committee must be representative, the programme must cover the training needs of all members and, ideally, the location of events should change so that members at the periphery are included.

How is relevance maintained? There is a danger that consortia can become inward looking and complacent. Regular analyses of training needs must be undertaken, and a watching brief maintained on best national and international practice. Finally, how is success measured? Although most training events and initiatives are evaluated there has been no study within the UK of the impact of co-operative staff development on training budgets, on staff retention and satisfaction, or, more importantly, on the quality of service at member libraries. This would be a valuable area of future research fitting particularly well with the current UK focus on assessing the benefits of collaborative working.

References

Academic and National Library Training Cooperative,
    www.anltc.ie/.
Avon University Libraries in Co-operation,
    www.uwe.ac.uk/library/info/aulic.htm.
Consortium of Academic Libraries in Manchester,
    www.calim.ac.uk/.
Consortium of Academic Libraries in Manchester Staff Training
    and Development Standing Committee (n.d.) *Policy for Staff
    Training and Development*,
    www.calim.ac.uk./text/traindev/trainpolicy.htm.

Cox, J. and Fallon, H. (2002) Staffing and Staff Development in Irish University Libraries, *SCONUL Newsletter*, **25**, 19–20.

CPD25 –Training and Development for HE Libraries in the London Region, www.cpd25.ac.uk/.

Evans, G. E. (2002) Management Issues of Co-operative Ventures and Consortia in the USA, Part One. *Library Management*, **23** (4/5), 213–26.

International Coalition of Library Consortia, www.library.yale.edu/consortia, index.html.

Joint Funding Councils' Libraries Review Group (1993) *Report* (The Follett Report), Higher Education Funding Council for England.

Joint M25 and University of London Staff Training and Development Group Review (2002) *Report of the Implementation Group*, www.M25lib.ac.uk/m25sec/docs/TIG_report.html.

M25 Consortium of Academic Libraries, www.M25lib.ac.uk/.

Mackenzie, A. (2002) Learning at Work: the CLIP Experience, *SCONUL Newsletter*, **25**, 15–17.

Peters, T. A. (2003) Consortia and Their Discontents, *Journal of Academic Librarianship,* **29** (2), 111–14.

Porter, G. (2001) Accrediting Staff Training and Development: CLIP – the CALIM Certificate in Library and Information Practice, *Personnel Training and Education*, **18** (1), 5–9.

Schneider, T. M. (2002) Academic Libraries and Regional Library Systems: how do they stand today?, *Journal of Academic Librarianship*, **28** (3), 141–6.

Scottish Academic Libraries Cooperative Training Group, www.jiscmail.ac.uk/files/LIS-SALCTG/welcome.html.

Sharpe, D. (2000) Pooled Expertise Lights the Way in Sunderland, *Public Library Journal*, **15** (2), 48–9.

Ulas, E. (2002) Scottish Academic Libraries Co-operative Training Group (SALCTG), *SCONUL Newsletter*, **25**, 18.

Wales Higher Education Libraries Forum, http://library.newport.ac.uk/whelf/.

10

Taking the strategic approach to staff development

Margaret Oldroyd

Introduction

The purpose of this chapter is threefold: to highlight some of the major issues that have been raised in the preceding chapters and to discuss some topics in more detail, to reflect on the current strategic role of staff development, and to make recommendations for future action on academic LIS workforce development.

Both the recent literature and experience suggest four important topics for consideration, and these have been highlighted by others in this book. First, what are the skills and competences that academic library staff will need for the future? Secondly, how are the competence maps and assessment tools that have been developed for the library and information services (LIS) sector helping with staff development planning? Thirdly, what use is being made of those increasingly important development routes: work-based learning and e-learning? Lastly, what are the best ways to develop management skills and, more specifically, leadership skills, in a wide range of academic library staff?

Skills for the future

A report from the Information Services National Training Organisation (ISNTO, 2003) shows that the library and information services sector believes that 44% of the skills that it requires for the future are already held by existing staff. The same report shows that the sector expects to meet 41% of its future skill needs by training existing staff or by recruiting new staff into the same posts. Another report, this time from Resource (Demos, 2003), points to the ageing working population and thus the problem with these assumptions, because a large number of our staff may be expected to retire in the next decade. Conversely, it may be argued that financial restraints are likely to result in a growing trend for staff to retire later than at present. In either case, libraries are faced with a staff development issue. Either there is a requirement to replace lost skills by training more staff in these skills from an earlier stage, or there is the question of staff, who in other times might have retired, being motivated and enabled to undertake development activities to ensure the currency of their skills. Libraries clearly need to have current information on the age profile and turnover rate of their staff, and of particular groups of staff, and to base their staff development plans and the scale of their programmes on the picture thus gained.

The Resource report further suggests that, while constraints of time and money do influence current levels of workforce development provision, 'increasing informed demand from both individuals and organizations is an essential part of helping improve supply'. So there is also an issue about proactivity in relation to staff development, both for organizations and for individuals.

The last few years have seen a great deal of project work and publication on the nature of the skills required by academic library staff now and in the future, some of which have been referred to in earlier chapters. Some relate to particular library functions and some to individual groups of staff, while others look more generally at skill needs across the board.

Jay Klagge at the University of Phoenix (1998) focuses on the skill needs of middle managers, which are seen to have increased as a result of the growth in team working, the quality movement, and 'a widespread incidence of organizational flattening'. Some of the new skills identified are: statistical measurement and customer service techniques, business process improvement procedures, coaching, consulting, partnering and facilitating. In particular, the abilities 'to lead from the middle, facilitate adaptability, unlock human diversity, develop individual team members and resolve group conflicts' are stressed, as are doing more through others and leading change 'through team-building, systems thinking and organizational visioning'.

The Association of Research Libraries, in a review of changing roles of library professionals (2000), picks up the theme of the changing skill needs resulting from redesigned jobs and structures in academic libraries and the influence of information technology. The latter is echoed in an Australian commentary on staff development and continuing professional development (Smith, 2002). In a survey of Australian university libraries, Smith found that increased use of IT in information services delivery had affected 91% of respondents' staff development programmes. Interestingly, 55% also reported increased use of IT in the delivery of staff development programmes such as computer-aided instruction. Writing from the Dutch perspective, Hans Geleijnse (1997) provides a case study in which new roles are seen as fundamental to the creation of the digital library at Tilburg University. He emphasizes the need for new skills in the areas of information management, user support and training, tailor-made services and electronic publishing. There is no doubt that IT continues to have enormous significance for the training needs of all academic library staff. They need to be 'at home' with the use of basic software packages. Senior managers must have an overview of its current uses and future potential. Each group of staff needs to be competent in using the specialist software, databases and so on that are relevant to their area of work. The key issue is that continuing development of new IT applications requires a planned and continuing programme of skills updating for all levels of staff. The appropriate use of IT as a means of delivering staff development is an area that libraries are now beginning to address in a new and more focused way, as illustrated in Moira Bent's chapter (Chapter 8).

Throughout this book reference has been made to the new skills required by academic library staff, with stress on different areas depending on the remit and view of the particular author. Role shift and role change have been constant themes in the preceding chapters, especially with reference to the networked environment, librarians as facilitators of learning, and the relative tasks and responsibilities of librarians and other LIS staff. Contributors to this book, together with many other published commentators, believe that change, and the consequent demand for new skills, will remain a constant feature of academic libraries and that staff development must, therefore, be a critical element in our change management strategies.

Competences maps and skills assessment tools

During the last few years there has been an upsurge in work in the UK on mapping LIS competences both across the sector and for particular groups and levels of staff. Some of this has resulted from government initiatives enacted via the ISNTO and some through projects. It may also be that a growing realization of the need for comprehensive training as a change management tool has led managers to wish to 'get a handle' on the scope of the skill areas to be covered.

Competences maps

The competences required of support staff in all types of libraries, at Levels 2, 3 and 4, have been mapped for the Information and Library Services National Vocational Qualifications (ILS NVQs), which Jo Webb discussed in Chapter 6. Interestingly, these bring together LIS, IT and customer service competences. The Level 2 and 3 functional and occupational maps were revised in 2002.

The ISNTO has conducted a major skills foresight project (ISNTO, 2003), which maps the competences required by staff under four major headings: external links (customers, research, fore-casting and influencing), job related (education, training, ICT and technical), management and personal. The project covers skills needed in the period 2003–7 and identifies priorities for training. It is interesting to note that people management and ICT figure highly in the list of the top twenty training needs, and generic management and personal skills are identified as key areas for training provision. The most urgent skill gaps are identified as marketing and promotion, supporting the learner and performance management. These priorities are derived from the whole LIS sector. In a related project (ISNTO, 2002), a toolkit is provided for individual libraries to conduct their own skills benchmarking to determine their own priorities. It would be interesting to know which academic libraries have done such an exercise and how the outcomes compare with the above findings for the sector.

A survey conducted by the Association of Research Libraries in the USA (ARL, 2002), sought to explore the status of core competences in research libraries and whether these libraries are defining or adopting them. Core competences were defined as 'the skills, knowledge, abilities and attributes that employees across an organization are expected to have to contribute successfully within a particular organizational context'. Slightly over a quarter of the 124 libraries surveyed have a map of core competences in place and the trend to adopt them is gaining momentum. In the majority of cases, the move to develop a map or list came from the library's management and in slightly over half the institutions an in-house list had been developed. Other respondents had adopted nationally published lists. The main reasons given for using the core competences lists are to clarify common goals, to identify skill gaps, and to develop training programmes. Only five libraries put a time limit on the acquisition of competence in core skills. The benefits for the library and the individual of using these lists are summarized as the clarity that they provide about performance expectations, and the consistent framework that they give for performance evaluation and the planning of training. A clear link can be seen here, as with the ISNTO benchmarking work discussed earlier, to providing tools that can be used in relation to the quality and performance management imperatives that are key issues for academic libraries.

Some libraries have created competences lists for particular areas of work, such as IT. Patricia Wallace (1999) describes using one of these before undertaking a major technology upgrade. She asked staff to rate themselves as 'mouseaphobic, mouseable, mouse-loving or mouse-master'! Staff were then trained to attain a set of mandatory core competences and they were also encouraged to attain a further set of intermediate competences.

The Hybrid Information Management: Skills for Senior Staff (HIMSS) project, as Pat Noon has discussed in Chapter 3, sought to identify a list of key skills required by heads or aspiring heads of academic library or converged services (Dalton and Nankivell, 2002). The project produced a list of generic management skills and personal attributes required of heads of service, which can be seen to constitute a map of these competences and has been developed further to provide an assessment tool. This HIMSS tool is the Learning Framework Online (n.d.) and it enables aspiring academic library leaders to plot and rate their skills and experience against those in the HIMSS list. The resulting report gives a skills profile and gap analysis enabling the individual to target necessary development areas.

Skills assessment tools

The TFPL Skills Toolkit (n.d.) is designed for the whole LIS sector and for all groups of staff. The user is asked to define their role as strategic, developmental or operational and then to compare their own knowledge and skills against lists of competences in six skills sets: management, people, personal, ICT, information management, and leadership.

The Chartered Institute of Library and Information Professionals (CILIP) provides two general tools, *The Framework for Continuing Professional Development* and *Turning Points: moving into management* (Library Association, 1992, 1998). The former is a tool that can be used by any member of staff at any point in their working life. It enables them to review their current skills and to assess their next career move and the training that they need to achieve it – the reflective practitioner approach. It groups skills and knowledge under four headings: library and information skills, personal effectiveness, management and corporate skills. *Turning Points* is for qualified librarians, with at least two to four years' experience, to use whenever they reach a turning point in their career, whether because of personal choice or external influences. It aims to help them to review 'their skills, knowledge, qualities and abilities to enable them to determine how to develop themselves and their careers'. Here there is a list of some of the skills that are recognized as useful to managers. *Turning Points* mixes personal, technical and management skills in no particular order and invites the individual to add to the list.

Klagge (1998) developed a list of 17 skill categories for middle managers at the University of Phoenix. This was divided into a list of seven major personal skill areas: personal communication, conflict resolution, leadership, consulting and facilitating, ethical and legal issues, developing and mentoring others and computing; and ten process skill categories: business process improvement, customer service, partnering, project management, mental models, systems thinking, change leadership, resource allocation, organizational visioning and navigating the organization. Klagge identified 120 specific skills as making up the broader categories. Managers were asked to assess the importance of each skill to the job, their current level of ability and the gap they needed to fill. Those with high importance ratings and low skill ratings formed the training agenda for current managers. Many of the examples described combine a competence map approach with self-assessment. Klagge has demonstrated an in-house approach to this for a particular group of staff.

Of course, there are advantages and disadvantages to the different methods. 'Off-the shelf' competence lists save time for the individual manager but may be less well attuned to the needs of a particular library. The lists that are developed by questioning staff will focus on needs as they see them, but may omit major skill needs because staff either have them already or do not perceive the need for them. It would certainly be interesting to know the experiences of UK academic librarians in using these tools, or their own 'home grown' ones, to understand better the skill sets and development needs of their staff.

Work-based learning and e-learning

Work-based learning

Another feature of recent writings on staff development for the LIS sector has been the attention paid to various forms of work-based learning, which are usefully summarised by Barbara Allan (1999). LIS graduates may well take up their first post having used the portfolio-building tool developed at Loughborough University (Beckett and Brine, 2002). The current presentation format for Chartership applications is a written statement and portfolio with an evaluative introduction. The growing tendency for staff to keep portfolios of evidence of their personal and professional development may well encourage more staff to think about the many activities that contribute to their learning and not just to focus on course attendance.

Mentoring and coaching are other methods that have been much written about. Byrne (2003) makes the useful point that: 'The beauty of mentoring is that it is not dependent on the willingness of your existing employer to support your development, although that obviously makes life easier.'

Howland (1999) has linked mentoring to the requirement to benefit from the skills of a more diverse workforce, and sees mentoring as the most successful way to keep these staff once they have been recruited. Mentoring and coaching have been especially recommended in relation to the development of senior managers, where the textbook becomes less useful and the sharing of experience and the opportunity to be guided through one's first attempts at complex assignments are especially valuable. Pat Noon touched on this earlier in relation to management development programmes (Chapter 3).

Paula T. Kaufman, Librarian of the University of Illinois at Urbana-Champaign, describes the intriguing idea of 'internal internships' as a means of encouraging more staff to go into academic library management (Kaufman, 2002). The individual is relieved of their normal duties for six to nine months to do project work and or shadow a library manager. Their posts provide job swap or job enrichment opportunities for other staff. Another idea is for one university to offer a similar programme to a librarian from another university.

In the Australian university libraries Smith (2002) reports that while conferences and both external and internal short courses are still the commonest staff development activities, a number of other methods are common. Publication and research are used by 44% and 38% of respondents respectively. These are methods for which encouragement by example from senior staff is vital. Internal job exchanges are used by 75% of respondents and 60% exchanged staff with other organizations. While there are known to be individual examples of both job swaps and staff exchanges in UK universities, it is doubtful that the practice is as widespread as in Australian universities or used in the systematic way, within and between institutions, described by Kaufman.

E-learning

Writing about the JULIA project at the library of the Technical University of Denmark, Bjørnshauge (1999) describes the use of various IT-based routes such as bulletin boards, electronic conferencing and discussion groups to empower the library staff to facilitate their own transition from a paper-based to a digital library. The library has provided all staff 'with their own work-station at home with access to the Internet, the Microsoft Office environment and other resources' and it pays the telecommunications costs. He comments: 'What has been accomplished is a self-supporting more or less autonomous training network, with activities planned and performed by the staff without much interference from the management.'

The Netskills programme in the UK and the ARL's Online Lyceum programme in the USA enable staff to learn at their own computers. The Danish experience differs in the level of autonomy in setting the training agenda that it appears to allow. Barbara Allan has provided a useful overview of the use of e-tools for LIS staff development, notably supporting induction and mentoring, and enabling them to become e-tutors and supporters of e-learning (1999; also 2002). These, and the approaches discussed earlier by Moira Bent (Chapter 8) and Sue White and Margaret Weaver (Chapter 7), may provide some answers to the problems that surround ensuring access to staff training opportunities for all members of academic library staff.

Management and leadership development

The development of library managers and leaders is a key issue for the future success of academic libraries. The Resource report referred to earlier in the chapter (Demos, 2003) states that leadership is the most frequently cited development need in its stakeholder survey. It stresses the need for a holistic approach to developing management and leadership skills across all groups of staff, but focuses particularly on the needs of current and aspiring service heads. Sheila Corrall (2002) has pointed out that coaching, developing others, networking, acting as a role model and creating a climate are skills that both managers and leaders need. This links back to the topic of work-based learning. Managers at all levels in our libraries will need the skills to mentor and coach others if this form of development is to be used more widely. The importance of leaders being able to manage people, to create and share a vision, and to build alliances within and outwith the library has been stressed earlier in this book.

Management skills and organizational change

These skills are also emphasized by David Orenstein (1999) in an article that focuses on the role of library managers in organizational transformation using a quality model. In his book on restructuring academic libraries to meet the needs of the future, Charles Schwartz (1997) cites a survey of American university libraries, which shows a very high level of organizational restructuring and an equal rise in the level of and expenditure on staff development. He sees change as situational (new site, new boss), and transition as the internal process that staff must go through to come to terms with change. It is this latter process for which leadership, including the skilled use of people management and staff development, is crucial. The same point is made in relation to the cultural changes that can be achieved through networked libraries (Reid and Foster, 2000). Purcell and Moore (2003) report on the ubiquitous nature of reorganization or restructuring in UK academic libraries, and the need for leaders who are skilled in organizational design and in initiating not just coping with change. It is clear, therefore, that there is a need to develop appropriate management and leadership skills in all staff, and that the leadership skills of current and future heads of service in the areas of visioning and people management are key to success in dealing with the constant changes and consequent transitions that staff must make.

Developing second-tier senior managers

An (unpublished) report about development for staff in second-tier senior management posts (the group that includes assistant heads, deputies and members of senior management teams) was prepared for the June 2003 meeting of the SCONUL (Society of College, National and University Libraries) Advisory Committee on Staffing, by Christine Fyfe (Librarian of Leicester University), Anne Murray (Deputy Librarian of Cambridge University) and this author. The report discusses the problems caused by the inability to assume a common level of management skills training prior to taking up, or in the early stages of being in, a second-tier post. It concludes that 'the issue is not the availability of suitable management skills courses but rather the lack of consistent participation in management skills development courses and activities across the sector'. It calls for management and leadership development to be key elements in academic libraries' strategic plans, together with the provision of financial and other resources to ensure consistent and equitable access to appropriate skills development for all staff. Were this recommendation to be taken up, all second-tier staff could be assumed to have a portfolio of accredited management skills so that the focus at second-tier level could be firmly on leadership development.

Leadership

The report goes on to discuss the distinction between management and leadership skills and concludes 'that there is a need for a new, high-level leadership development programme' for the academic libraries sector, with agreed selection criteria and transparent selection processes. This reflects the increasing provision of leadership programmes in a number of other countries. The ARL programmes (www.arl.org) and the Frye Leadership Institute (www.fryeinstitute.org) in the USA, and the Aurora Foundation Programme in Australia (www.alia.org. au/aurora/aurora.html), are notable examples. While many of these programmes involve an intensive taught course element or exposure to a range of high level speakers, they also use methods such as mentoring, coaching, projects, secondments, 360 degree assessment and the formation of peer group networks. This agrees with points made earlier about the value of work-based learning and the need for a mix of approaches which is confirmed by the HIMSS project (Dalton and Nankivell, 2002). The new Leadership Foundation described in Chapter 1 potentially has a key role here.

Succession planning

Angela Bridgland, Deputy Librarian at the University of Melbourne, draws on management literature and her own experience in writing a human resource plan for her library, to discuss succession planning and succession management in academic libraries, a topic that she notes is hardly covered in the literature (Bridgland, 1999, 23).

The challenge is to make succession planning more germane to current work practices in which teams are emphasised and leadership responsibilities shared. Rather than focussing on the right person for the right position at the right time, organisations need to develop strong leadership teams for strategic tasks. Leading an organisation requires a wide range of skills, knowledge and talents resident in more than one person and in more than one level of the organisation.

By developing the appropriate skills in a wide range of staff, the library ensures 'depth in its leadership capability at all levels' to support the flatter management structures that are now so prevalent. It enables libraries to 'grow their own' potential strategic leaders by supporting them to develop the skills that they will need in the future, and it avoids the pitfalls that can surround attempts to focus too sharply on replacements for specific posts or on individuals. Bridgland also highlights the importance of mentoring: 'Senior managers need to endorse mentoring as a legitimate development strategy designed to accelerate career development.' Clearly, she agrees with Pat Noon on the challenges facing individual academic libraries, and the sector, about the development of current middle and senior managers, about enabling them to support the development of the managers and leaders of the future and about the new emphasis on dealing with change by developing skills and competences in depth rather than focusing on development for current tasks and posts.

The role of staff development in library human resource management

Management responsibility

In a previous publication this author advocated the need for libraries to have a senior manager with responsibility for staff development as part of a wider human resource management (HRM) brief (Oldroyd, 1996). A recent check through the SCONUL senior management team lists reveals that 88% of those responsible for staff development are senior management team members. At least 12% (20) institutions have a senior manager with a portfolio explicitly linking staff development to human resource management and other strategic issues. (There may be others but the lists are unclear.) Post titles vary: deputy librarian (support services), sub-librarian planning and administration, sub-librarian strategy and planning, assistant director staff development, service development manager, assistant director resource management, staff and service development manager, staff and quality development manager. An e-mail survey of the 20 post-holders revealed that, of the 11 who responded, all the posts had been created in the last five years and most of them in the last two. It is very encouraging to note this recent change, which indicates that staff development and HRM may be moving into a more central and strategic position as evidenced in management structures.

Respondents testified to their belief in staff development as integral to the HRM brief and to delivery of strategic aims. Two examples provide views from an old and a new university.

> I see staff development as a major part of my strategy and planning role. Like most university libraries, half our budget goes on staff, so they are a key resource and critical to the quality of service we provide … I think having an overarching responsibility at senior level is critically important, so that the broadest perspective on the whole HRM picture is maintained.

> Human resource management is a major aspect of my role, as is developing services, implementing change and planning for the future. Effective staff development is crucial to these areas.

The types of responsibilities that make up the rest of the portfolio include performance measurement, quality assurance, planning, marketing and PR. In most cases, the individual is also responsible for HRM ranging from selection and recruitment, appraisal and disciplinary issues to succession planning and staff contracts.

Links to quality management

The links between service quality, effective HRM and staff development, which have always been there, are beginning to be overtly recognized through the creation of roles that encompass them and by including them in strategic goals. A couple of examples show how this can enable these synergies to be exploited to good effect. At De Montfort University, the opportunity offered by the closure of one campus, and the merging of its stock and staff with those at another campus, has been used to enable all staff involved to participate in a marketing training day, of which the result was a marketing plan for the project and a wider understanding among staff of the role of a marketing approach in ensuring service quality. Another example has been the use of process improvement projects resulting from customer survey results, to enable staff to acquire skills in process improvement techniques.

Library human resource plans

It would appear that library human resource (HR) plans are in their infancy in the UK. None of the respondents to the e-mail survey had library HR plans, although two were expecting to develop one, and all mentioned general library strategic plans in which HR and staff development were included. De Montfort University Library's HR plan covers structure and role design, skills profile (numbers, audit and gaps), staff development and training, communication, health and safety, retention, progression and reward, performance management, leadership development and succession planning. It maps strategic goals and annual objectives against the seven key results areas in the library's strategic plan. Australian university libraries have longer experience in this area. Study of three examples of Australian academic library HR plans informed the design of the De Montfort plan. However, UK academic libraries may find themselves having to catch up in this area as pressure from HEFCE for the creation of institutional HR plans is beginning to result in individual departments being asked to 'follow suit'.

This should be seen as an excellent opportunity to map out strategic and operational staffing and staff development goals, which can then be used in making the case both within and outwith the library for the necessary resources to deliver them.

Staff development policies, annual development plans, programmes and evaluative reports, job and person specifications for all posts that show clear development criteria for progression are some of the other ways in which staff development can be fully embedded in the strategic processes of the library. It would take research such as that undertaken by Ian W. Smith (2002) for Australian academic libraries to assess how far these things are in place in UK academic libraries and elsewhere.

Performance measurement and staff development

Another indicator of the increasing strategic importance accorded to staff development by UK academic libraries is the growing number of them that have achieved Investors in People (IiP) status (www.investorsinpeople.co.uk). This is a national standard, based on the four principles of commitment, planning, action and evaluation, which provides 12 indicators by which any organization can benchmark the quality of its staff development processes, and the degree to which they are supporting the achievement of its aims and objectives. Paterson testifies to the value of the external assessment involved in achieving IiP recognition:

> ... the exercise focused minds at all levels on the problem of professional skills and knowledge, and provided a framework for analysis and action, encouraged better measurement methods for performance improvement, demonstrated the value put on staff effort by management and offered a snapshot of morale, communications, perspectives at all levels. All of which moved us down the road towards an ultimate goal – becoming the kind of organisation where learning is habitual and where, crucially, people are empowered to invest in themselves as the hybrid library goes through its changes (Paterson, 1999).

The new IiP Profile provides a grading system for the standard for use by recognized organizations. It has three sections: developing our strategy, implementing our strategy and developing our people. It has 23 measures and four levels for each measure. When sufficient organizations have used it, a benchmarking service is to be launched enabling individual organizations to compare their 'scores' with average results. The recent development of optional IiP models for specific staff development areas such as leadership and management provides another tool for measuring staff development activities. The development of the IiP internal assessment model, for example at Coventry University, provides another means of embedding development and quality enhancement skills.

There are currently no agreed performance indicators for staff development in UK academic libraries nor, to this author's knowledge, do they exist elsewhere. The question of whether a set of indicators should be developed is a topic currently being looked at by the SCONUL Advisory Committees on Performance Indicators and on Staffing. The Learning and Skills Council (2002) has suggested 11 indicators for employer engagement in workforce development, and it would be interesting to see how well these would suit the sector.

Recommendations for the future

General

The many projects previously cited have firmly established that all library staff, librarians and support staff need technical (LIS and IT), personal and management skills. Any well thought out staff development programme needs to address all three areas, with only the balance between them and the detailed skill needs altering according to the group or individual concerned. This provides an established starting-point, which should be used by individuals, staff development managers and the sector to underpin a comprehensive approach to provision.

There is a need for more understanding of what constitutes best practice in relation to academic library staff development and enhancement of the ability to make meaningful comparisons at national and international levels. A survey of current staff development practice in academic libraries, covering the same areas as Smith's Australian study (2002) and including use and results of tools such as IiP, competences maps and skills assessment tools, carried out in the UK and in other countries, would be a valuable starting-point. The outcomes could be used to disseminate good practice, facilitate benchmarking and enable international comparisons.

The creation and agreement of performance indicators for academic library staff development can usefully be promoted by bodies such as SCONUL working in partnership with CILIP groups and the regional training groups. SCONUL can also do much to disseminate and encourage adoption of best practice ideas.

The contributors to this book have made it clear that successful academic staff development requires a coherent and consistent approach to workforce development at four levels: individual staff member, individual library, region and sector.

The individual employee level

The Resource report (Demos, 2003) states: 'it is the sectoral workforce itself that will ultimately decide its own future' and this is a timely reminder that, in this era of portfolio careers, individual employees need to be proactive throughout their working life in assessing their needs and skills, and planning, participating in and recording their development achievements.

The organizational level

Heads of service need to ensure that their libraries have HR plans that identify the role of staff development in achieving their goals and encompass the issue of succession planning.

A senior manager, preferably with responsibility for HR and quality issues as well as staff development, helps to ensure that the vital links between these areas are made and that they are systematically and coherently managed. The use of competences maps, skills assessment tools, review and appraisal systems, and benchmarking frameworks such as those provided by IiP aid the latter task.

The provision of sound management training for all managers, especially the development of HRM skills, and the enhanced use of work-based learning, e-learning, mentoring and coaching, are key challenges and there is much to be learned in some of these areas from colleagues in the USA and Australia.

Clear job and person specifications, including the skills and qualifications criteria for progression, and skills training that covers the three core areas cited above, for all staff, are other key requirements. To achieve all this and to 'grow' the academic library leaders of the future, the oft spoken belief in staff being an institution's most important resource will need to be backed up by the allocation of appropriate amounts of time and money to their development.

The regional level

The kinds of regional consortia surveyed in the last chapter have a vital role to play in enabling provision that could not be supported by individual libraries. Many could extend their role by setting up a coherent programme of job swaps, shadowing and mentoring between institutions so that these opportunities are available to all regardless of geographic location. Another potential role is suggested by Moira Bent (Chapter 8), that of sharing the creation, dissemination and use of electronic learning materials.

These groups could also establish fruitful links with the regional agencies, some of which have already appointed workforce development officers, taking on a wider remit as advocates for the training needed in particular places. Together with CILIP groups and branches, they provide a potential local vehicle for a more strategic sector approach to delivering staff development, for sharing good practice, and benchmarking.

However, regional training co-operatives depend for their effectiveness on the full engagement of all local academic libraries through equal effort and or appropriate financial contributions. Research into their effectiveness in promoting service quality, as suggested by Philippa Dolphin (Chapter 9), could help to strengthen perceptions of their strategic role.

The sectoral level

At this level, coherent working between relevant government and professional bodies is key to ensuring that the training needs of the academic libraries sector are well understood. In the UK, a close working relationship between the new Sector Skills Council, which is responsible for the development of the information services workforce, and CILIP and SCONUL is needed.

In the USA and in Australia, academic librarians are able to access appropriate leadership development programmes. In Chapter 3 Pat Noon has eloquently demonstrated that, in the UK, enough time has been spent on defining the skills and competences required. The need now is for coherent provision and comprehensive take-up, for a significant shift in culture in relation to succession planning and support. SCONUL can play a key role in making sure that a new, high level leadership development programme is available to appropriate staff, for example, through liaison with the new Leadership Foundation, and that this draws on good practice established in the USA and Australia.

The academic LIS sector must work diligently to ensure that, at long last, there is coherent, consistent support for certificated development of all support staff through ILS NVQs or other comparable routes, following the good practice examples that several contributors, especially Jo Webb in Chapter 6, have described. But this is also a matter of providing real support, involving the allocation of time and money, and of the need for a change in culture and attitude among some of those with the ability to unlock these resources, and whose responsibility it is actively to enable the development of their staff.

Conclusion

A proactive approach to staff development is needed at all four of the levels described above. In many instances this means joint activity at more than one level on the same thing. The individual employee must take an active role in planning their own CPD, including taking up relevant opportunities, which the employer must provide. While an appropriate leadership programme can only be negotiated at sector level, positive support in terms of time, money and example must be given by current heads of service. Potential candidates must participate with enthusiasm and regional groups must both promote the programme and support participants, for example, through exchanges and action learning sets. The University of Melbourne Library's Human Resources Plan (Bridgland, 1999) talks about 'closing the gap between its current performance and its strategic intent'. Future success for academic library staff and their libraries depends on active recognition by everyone in the sector that the gap cannot be closed without a strategically managed approach to staff development.

References

Allan, B. (1999) *Developing Information and Library Staff through Work-based Learning*, London, Library Association Publishing.

Allan, B. (2002) *E-learning and Teaching in Library and Information Services, London, Facet Publishing.*

Association of Research Libraries (2000) *Changing Roles of Library Professionals*, SPEC Kit 256, Washington, ARL.

Association of Research Libraries (2002) *Core Competences*, SPEC Kit 270, Washington, ARL.

Beckett, I. and Brine, A. (2002) *Recording Skills Development for Information and Library Science*, Loughborough, Learning and

Teaching Support Network – Information and Computer Sciences.

Bjørnshauge, L. (1999) Reengineering Library Services: human resource management, *Serials*, **12** (2), 139–42.

Bridgland, A. (1999) To Fill, or How to Fill – That is the Question: succession planning and leadership development in academic libraries, *Australian Academic and Research Libraries*, **30** (1), 20–9.

Byrne, D. (2003) Mentoring, Enabling, Empowering, Inspiring, *Library & Information Update*, **2** (4), 38–9.

Corrall, S. (2002) *Developing Library Leaders: a management responsibility*. Paper given at the Public Libraries Authorities Conference, Chester, 15–18 October, www.cilip.org.uk/about/president/corralls/president_106.rtf.

Dalton, P. and Nankivell, C. (2002) *Hybrid Information Management: skills for senior staff HIMSS*, Birmingham, Centre for Information Research, University of Central England, www.himss.bham.ac.uk/researchdocuments.html.

Demos (2003) *Towards a Strategy for Workforce Development*, London, Resource.

Geleijnse, H. (1997) Human Resource Management and the Digital Library, *International Journal of Electronic Library Research*, **7** (1), 25–42.

Howland, J. (1999) Beyond Recruitment: retention and promotion strategies to ensure diversity and success, *Library Administration and Management*, **13** (1), 4–14.

Information Services National Training Organisation (2002) *In-house Skills Benchmarking: toolkit and supporting notes*, Bradford, ISNTO.

Information Services National Training Organisation (2003) *Skills Foresight in the Information Services Sector 2003 2009*, Bradford, ISNTO.

Kaufman, P. T. (2002) *Where Do the Next 'We' Come From? Recruiting, retaining, and developing our successors*, ARL

Bimonthly Report 221, Washington, DC, Association of Research Libraries.

Klagge, J. (1998) Self-perceived Development Needs of Today's Middle Managers, *Journal of Management Development*, **17** (7), 481–91.

Learning and Skills Council (2002) *Workforce Development Strategy*, London, HMSO.

Learning Framework Online, www.himss-lfo.bham.ac.uk/.

Library Association (1992) *The Framework for Continuing Professional Development*, London, Library Association.

Library Association (1998) *Turning Points: moving into management*, London, Library Association.

Oldroyd, M. (ed.) (1996) *Staff Development in Academic Libraries*, London, Library Association Publishing.

Orenstein, D. (1999) Developing Quality Managers and Quality Management, *Library Administration and Management*, **13** (1), 44–51.

Paterson, A. (1999) Ahead of the Game: developing academic library staff for the twenty-first century. In International Association of Technological University Libraries, *The Future of Libraries in Human Communications*, IATUL, 19–26.

Purcell, J. and Moore, K. (2003) A Change for the Better – making organisational change work for your library, *Relay*, **55** (July), 13–16.

Reid, B. J. and Foster, W. (2000) *Achieving Cultural Change in Networked Libraries*, Aldershot, Gower.

Schwartz, C. (1997) *Restructuring Academic Libraries*, Chicago, Association of College and Research Libraries.

Smith, I. W. (2002) *Staff Development and Continuing Professional Education Policy and Practice in Australian Academic and Research Libraries*. IFLA Satellite Meeting, Aberdeen, www.lib.latrobe.edu.au/publications/.

TFPL Skills Toolkit, http://skillstoolkit.tfpl.com/.

Wallace, P. ((1999) Hurtling through Cyberspace: tackling technology training, *Computers in Libraries*, **19** (2), 20–6.

Index